CONVERSATIONS THAT SELL

Conversations That Sell
Collaborate with Buyers and Make Every Conversation Count

NANCY BLEEKE

AMACOM

American Management Association

New York • Atlanta • Brussels • Chicago • Mexico City • San Francisco
Shanghai • Tokyo • Toronto • Washington, D. C.

Bulk discounts available. For details visit:
www.amacombooks.org/go/specialsales
Or contact special sales:
Phone: 800-250-5308
E-mail: specialsls@amanet.org
View all the AMACOM titles at: www.amacombooks.org
American Management Association: www.amanet.org

This publication is designed to provide accurate and authoritative information in regard to the subject matter covered. It is sold with the understanding that the publisher is not engaged in rendering legal, accounting, or other professional service. If legal advice or other expert assistance is required, the services of a competent professional person should be sought.

Library of Congress Cataloging-in-Publication Data

Bleeke, Nancy.
   Conversations that sell : collaborate with buyers and make every conversation count / Nancy Bleeke.
      p. cm.
   Includes bibliographical references and index.
   ISBN 978-0-8144-3180-1
   1. Selling. 2. Customer relations. 3. Sales management. I. Title.
   HF5438.25.B5653 2013
   658.85—dc23   2012028042

About AMA

American Management Association (www.amanet.org) is a world leader in talent development, advancing the skills of individuals to drive business success. Our mission is to support the goals of individuals and organizations through a complete range of products and services, including classroom and virtual seminars, webcasts, webinars, podcasts, conferences, corporate and government solutions, business books and research. AMA's approach to improving performance combines experiential learning—learning through doing—with opportunities for ongoing professional growth at every step of one's career journey.

Printing number
10 9 8 7 6 5 4 3 2 1

CONTENTS

PART I
Selling in Today's Transparent World

v

PART II
The What and How of Collaborative Sales Conversations

9 Facilitate, Part II: Work Through Objections 143

10 Then Consolidate: Close Every Conversation with Purpose 161

PART III
The Factors That Make or Break Your Sales

Today's buyers have changed, fundamentally and forever. They spend countless hours online researching their issues and challenges. They're highly knowledgeable about the numerous options available and see minimal difference between them.

Sound familiar? It's because we're all doing it these days. We bounce from website to website, learning as much as we can about the problems we're facing. We search for how others are solving them and what resources are available. We find out what others think of the various products, services, and companies we're considering.

Then we're finally ready to talk to a salesperson. But our guard is up. We don't want to be sold.

Neither do our customers. They detest product-pushing peddlers. When listening to our messages or reading our emails, they take great pleasure in deleting us as fast as they can. When we meet with them they're in self-protection mode, waiting for our inevitable pitch and pressure to take action.

This scenario is a recipe for disaster. We're trying hard to sell. We're asking about their budgets and decision-making process. We're touting our features and capabilities. And we're going nowhere fast.

Here's the deal. To be successful in sales, you need to get in much earlier—even before your prospects are considering making a change. You also need fresh sales strategies that actually work in this volatile business environment. Today's crazy-busy prospects expect so much more from you. They want you to be both a valuable resource and to collaborate with them to help them achieve their objectives.

This isn't about selling. No one wants to be sold anymore. It's about leveraging your offering, the research you've done, your previous experience, and your customer's knowledge to help them get where they want to go. When you do that, they want to work with you—and will even pay more for the opportunity.

And that's exactly why this book is so darn important. When I first met Nancy Bleeke, we talked about her "Genuine Sales" training course. Of course, the title itself stood out in stark contrast to the manipulative sales techniques taught by the old-school gurus.

When I asked her about it, she said, "It's about being real with your customers. So many salespeople hide behind their products and services. They think that's what matters. But it's not. People want to work with you because of what you bring to the relationship."

Bingo! She hit the truth head on. That's all today's prospects want. To back that up, check out the results of a recent survey by the Corporate Executive Board (CEB) of 6000+ corporate decision makers regarding what they valued most in their sales reps. The single greatest contributor (53 percent) to customer loyalty was sales experience. This led to their reps being able to offer them unique perspectives, educate them, and help them to reduce risk and make tough choices. Notice that it's nothing about the product, service, or price.

Further CEB studies showed that reps who exhibited these same qualities in conversations with new prospects were significantly more successful than those who didn't. Notice again that it's all about you, your knowledge, and how you leverage it.

That's the good news too. While you can't do much to influence your company's offering, market position, or pricing, you have 100 percent control over you. Every bit of time and effort you invest in yourself has a lifelong impact. It's something you can take with you, no matter what direction your career goes.

So let's get serious about what really counts. It all comes down to the conversations that you have with your prospects. Will they capture their attention and pique their curiosity? Or will they be mundane and forgettable? Will they showcase you as a person who could bring value? Or will you sound like every other self-serving salesperson?

In this book, Nancy Bleeke does an excellent job of showing you what it takes to have those collaborative, engaging conversations—whether the conversation is an initial meeting with new prospects to sell them on your value or a meeting with existing customers to uncover new ways to help them.

As for getting by on your natural charm, that's simply not enough today. Instead, you'll learn how to augment it with a planning process that leverages your pre-call research and your personal expertise.

Yes, you'll be investing more time upfront getting ready, but it will be well worth it. Your meetings will go so much better because you've changed your focus. You'll need fewer prospects to meet your quota. And your sales cycles will be much faster—all because "right-sizing" your efforts and conversations for each prospect allows you to be smarter with your time and energy.

By embracing these strategies, you're on your way to success. You're going to need to practice, though. Learning new skills always takes time and feels awkward at first. But the upside is so worth it.

The choice is yours. You can continue down the path you've been on, working harder and harder to achieve your goals. Or you can decide to excel with *Conversations that Sell*!

—Jill Konrath, **author of** *SNAP Selling* and *Selling to Big Companies*

ACKNOWLEDGMENTS

My career and life have been blessed by many people who support, challenge, learn, grow, and celebrate with me. Were it not for them, this book would never have been written. There would be no lessons learned or inspiration to share with you.

First among them are the people in sales, with whom I am deeply honored to work each day. Thank you to each and every one of you. Partnering with you has deepened my passion to help others sell well and feel good about their profession. I have learned from you, cheered you on, and celebrated your successes. I continue to wish you the best in all you do.

"Mentor" doesn't begin to describe the wonderful guides, encouragers, and teachers I have had in my career. My heartfelt thanks go to the inspiring and ubiquitous Jill Konrath, who has forged a path for many sales experts to share what we know and give, give, give to each other, the sales community, and the world. She is my motivation for getting this book in print. I also thank Sharon Ellis, Bill Koeper, Peter Reynolds, and Ron Willingham who have played vital roles in building my belief in the profession of selling.

To my family, who is along for a wild ride with me around, thank you. My husband, Jon, who brings the stability to our home that allows me freedom to explore my ideas and endeavors. Our children, Kevin, Jackson, and Jenna, are a never-ending source of joy—and challenges. My aspirations for your well-being motivate me to keep learning and becoming a better person.

To my parents, who are no longer here in body, but whose spirits live in my work ethic, my desire to do the right thing, and my belief that I could "fall into a bucket of dung and come out smelling like a rose." Their belief in me has kept me taking chances and seeking adventures.

To my brothers, Joe, Bill, Phillip, and Shawn Noel, whose goading spurs me on to tackle and achieve even more, thank you. To my sister, Collette Pleva, thank you for your sympathetic ear and occasional kick in the pants to get things done. And thanks to my dear cousin, Lena Bredin, who is always interested in and supportive of my work.

Heaps of admiration go to my long-time business collaborators who have become dear friends: Kristine Amara, Ed Baron, Melissa Blair, Maggi Franks, Julie Kaye, Leslie Lynch, Patrice McGuire, Gloriann Perque, and Anne Stein. To Kayla Kutz, thank you for slogging through the early and scattered stages of putting the proposal together. Lynn Zimmer, your positive support, guidance, and "tough messages" over the years have made all I do better, thank you. Alice Kemper who has added depth and clarity to many of the sales best practices—thanks for collaborating and sharing your expertise. And thanks to Noreen Carballo whose positive and energetic force in the office kept me on track when I needed it.

My deep appreciation and respect go to the many sales and marketing experts I admire: Ardath Albee, Jeb Blount, Danita Bye, Jonathan Farrington, Colleen Francis, Lynn Hidy, Kendra Lee, Paul McCord, Anne Miller, Nancy Nardin, Jeanette Nyden, Lori Richardson, Steven Rosen, Clayton Shold, and Colleen Stanley.

Thank you to my dearest friends, who see all my quirks, let me be "me," and seem to enjoy my company anyway: Risa Feinstein, Amy Kutz, Connie Schreib, Shelly Schroeder, and Kara Whittow.

For the professional editors who helped me streamline and clarify my message, I am deeply grateful: Paul Simon of Sharper Content; Bob Nirkind, Senior Acquisitions Editor at AMACOM; Debbie Posner of Fluent in English, who collaboratively worked through final edits in a positive and energetic fashion; Michael Sivilli and his team at AMACOM who shepherded this book to print; and a special lady, Janice Bowen of the Department of Creativity, who helped me over the first big hurdle in getting started.

A huge thank-you to the graphics experts who, over many years, have helped me refine and clarify the graphics and tools used throughout the book, Dana Kader-Robb of Barefoot Marketing and Jeanette Pham of Sosh—your abilities to continue to elevate my ideas into usable aids is invaluable.

And finally, to my clients, thank you for the endeavors we've tackled together. I am honored to be welcomed into your companies to share ideas, best practices, and amazing results.

CONVERSATIONS THAT SELL

Did you choose a sales career? Not many people do. Most study disciplines such as engineering, teaching, accounting, business, or law, and then find themselves in sales not by choice, rather out of necessity, or because sales responsibilities have been thrown into their current job. I sure didn't want to be in sales.

I've spent my career working with salespeople, and yet for the first dozen years, I really didn't want to be one of them. I didn't think of myself as "in sales" and didn't want others to view me that way. I didn't want to be thought of in those derogatory terms that people are quick to conjure up, like: sales weasel, used car salesman, manipulator, and sleazy sales guy. I wanted to be a business professional, not a saleswoman.

While I didn't consider myself in sales, I worked with salespeople every day. I hired and trained hundreds of sellers—meaning that I have interviewed and talked with thousands in the profession. In those conversations, I learned that my reaction and reluctance to being in sales is shared by many, even those with "sales" in their job titles.

Why is it that so few willingly choose the profession or even accept that they are in sales? Why do the negative stereotypes persist? Why do my young adult children and their friends look at me like I have green skin and horns when I suggest they consider a career in sales?

One reason is that old perceptions linger—not only in sitcoms and in the minds of irritated customers, but surprisingly within sales organizations. All too often, the sales team is viewed negatively. They are viewed as, "those people who don't keep regular hours, who don't have to follow the rules, who get to travel and don't have to sit behind a desk all day; those people who are irritatingly demanding about getting their customers what they want and need."

Because I work with so many ethical sales professionals throughout the world, I find it surprising that these negative connotations linger on. And I see the impact of this negativity on sellers every day. It shows up in the way they put off prospecting and contacting buyers, in increased stress, discomfort, and fear.

Hardworking, professional people are even willing to quit their companies and their jobs when asked to take on sales as part of their responsibilities. I call them reluctant sellers. The reluctance stems from many sources: they don't know what to do, they're embarrassed to be in sales, they don't want to manipulate others for personal gain, or they believe it's not a viable career choice.

For many years, I was one of them.

Growing up in Kenosha, Wisconsin, a blue-collar town where manufacturing plants such as American Motors, Jockey International, and Ocean Spray were plentiful, I didn't know many people in sales. There was my Uncle Vince, who was a "businessman," and then there was Louie, our insurance agent.

I admired Louie, who always had a smile on his face and was the first person we called as my five siblings and I each got our driver's license. I saw him ease my mom's concerns when a storm destroyed the shell of our hand-built, first-ever garage. Within a week, a professional crew of carpenters rebuilt the garage with new lumber. In my eyes, he was a hero in our time of need. Yet my dad, a "union man," called him "Louie, the thief." And that definition of a salesperson is what stuck.

When recruiters came to my college campus to find candidates for "marketing jobs," I knew what they were really looking for—salespeople. Not wanting to be known as "Nancy, the thief," I didn't even consider those opportunities. Instead, I chose a career in human resources, where I could put my business and psychology training to work.

My beliefs about salespeople were further reinforced in my first job, when I was asked to coordinate the relocation of our sales team. I was advised to carefully scrutinize each seller's expenses, with the implication that these "sales guys" would try to push through expenses they shouldn't. They couldn't be trusted.

Fast forward ten years through several promotions and company moves while earning my MBA. I was the head of HR and Training at a toy distribution company. To my surprise, the president, Peter Reynolds, thoroughly embraced sales. His love of sales, his encouragement to explore new skills and responsibilities, combined with the freedom he extended to fail if you simply tried, began to change my ingrained perceptions.

It was a slow process to dispel lifelong negative thoughts about the value of sales. Though I had been a top-tier fundraiser since I was seven, had a newspaper route where I sold subscriptions, and even sold jewelry, I still had a hard time accepting that I was a salesperson.

When I did, my career possibilities, comfort level, and success exploded.

After working closely with the toy company's sales team, hiring a national sales force, coaching sales managers, and finding training for the sellers that confirmed selling is a value-filled profession, I took a leap of faith and put my burgeoning sales skills to work as an independent consultant.

Within a month, a former colleague connected me to a huge sales opportunity. And the rest, as they say, is history. Since 1998 I've been able to build a profitable and valuable training and consulting firm by selling my services and solutions, ironically specializing in sales!

As I changed my beliefs about sales, I realized that we are all "in sales." Whether we are selling products or services to customers in exchange for money; or are nontraditional sellers who sell ideas or ourselves; or influence others within the companies we work for, within our families, within our places of worship, social circles, or communities—we are all in sales. I was in sales as an HR Manager selling jobs, opportunities, our company, myself, policies, and ideas. It was then that I realized I wanted to change the negativity surrounding sales and help others become successful sellers.

I wrote this book, not only to share best practices; I wrote it to shatter the damaging clichés about salespeople. I want people to see that they don't need to be intimidated by sales or turn themselves into someone else to succeed. On the contrary, effective selling is about having meaningful, collaborative conversations where you, the buyer, and your companies win, and where you are an important part of your solution.

I want people to know that the skills to be successful in sales can be learned and the will to do so can be ignited.

If you aren't a "born salesperson"—and very few are—this book is for you. If you're tired of painful trial-and-error experiences, this book is for you. The tools, ideas, and formulas found in it will shorten your learning curve, improve your probability of success, increase your close rates, and help you capture repeat and larger sales.

This book is also written for those considering the sales profession as well as for those who have chosen sales and want to improve; for people who have had sales imposed on them and don't believe they have what it takes; for contented sellers who are embarrassed to admit they like their jobs; and for people who need to persuade others to accept ideas and take action—and that's all of us, isn't it?

Whether you are in B2B, B2C, or nontraditional sales, this book is full of information to help you:

- Sell collaboratively.

- Make every conversation count.

- Approach your sales conversations with a "What's in it for Them" (WiifT) mindset.

- Realize the power of the triple-win—Win^3—where you, your client, and both your companies win.

- Address Problems, Opportunities, Wants, and Needs (POWNs).

- Build your Skill and Will for sales success.

What you won't find in this book are chapters about value propositions or lead generation. These topics are well covered by other authors. You won't find a "be like me" message, either. I won't tell you exactly what to say, or suggest you follow a word-for-word script for your sales conversations. There are no exact words that work in every conversation. Each is as unique as the people involved in it.

Instead, I'll outline concepts, formulas, and thought-starters compiled from the best practices I've observed in top producers around the world—practical tips and ideas you can easily adapt into your own words, for your own customer base, and your industry, making your conversations comfortable and natural for you and each buyer.

A sales approach that is consistent yet flexible, adapted to those involved, and focused on mutual gain is what forms trust, builds confidence in you and your solution, and closes sales. That's what you'll find in this book.

You have permission to use any of the ideas you find in these pages, although I strongly encourage you to make them your own. Access the tools in downloadable form at www.conversationsthatsell.com, where you will also find additional resources and helpful links.

WHAT YOU WILL FIND IN THIS BOOK

Conversations That Sell shows you the "what" and "how" of successful sales conversations and provides you with the information and tools you need to take action. It also addresses the "why" of sales success, so you can embrace your sales role and give higher value to anyone who has the privilege of having a conversation with you. You'll learn how to make every interaction count for them and yourself. And you'll learn how to work smarter . . . not harder.

Part I: Selling in Today's Transparent World sets the stage for the best practices, skills, tools, and drivers of sales success. You will discover:

- The importance of you in the selling process.

- The Win^3 of success.

- What buyers in today's transparent selling environment need from you.

- Why collaborative selling is valuable.

Part II: The What and How of Collaborative Sales Conversations introduces the actions, formulas, and models that will make your conversations count. You will find the how-to's that:

- Guide you through productive collaborative conversations with a five-step sales system.

- Help you identify and adapt your approach to your buyer's type using the Tribal Types model.

- Guarantee you will move through your conversation efficiently to advance or close the sale.

- Prepare for relevant and timely sales conversations.

- Open a conversation that engages your buyer and earns you the right to move forward.

- Uncover sales opportunities by investigating the problems, opportunities, wants, and needs of your buyer.

- Facilitate value-filled presentations of your solution matched to the buyer.

- Work through objections as a problem resolver to reduce discounting and delays.

- Capture the buy decision and advance the sale more quickly.

- Make yourself valuable as you focus on What's in it for Them.

Part III: The Factors that Make or Break Your Sales provides the information and tools that support strengthening your will to succeed. These are the components missing in many sales books. You will learn about:

- The Success Drivers™ model that explains why you do or don't take the actions needed for sales success.

- The tools you need in your sales toolbox.

- An easy, yet effective, goal achievement process that will guide you in setting, planning for, and achieving your goals.

I suggest you read the book without judgment, bias, or assumptions. Read it first as an overview. Read it to familiarize yourself with the concepts, tools, models, and framework for conversations. Then spend time digesting each chapter so you can put the ideas into action.

Each chapter ends with "Quick Tips"—actions you can easily incorporate into your sales conversations and practices.

As a sales and training professional, I work hard in my workshops and courses to support and encourage participants to try, tweak, and learn what does and doesn't work for them. Unfortunately, a book cannot provide the personal support or accountability for application and practice that you get in a training session, so it's up to you to identify the ideas and tools you will commit to put into practice.

If you want accountability to adopt and use the information and tools, build it in with your stakeholders as you set goals using the process outlined in Chapter 13.

Long-term sales success is an ongoing journey, and I congratulate you for investing your time in seeking ways to strengthen your skill and will to succeed. I believe that if you apply and adapt the ideas in this book, you will not only be a more successful seller, you will also feel much better about what you do. You will have the confidence and competence to make every conversation count!

PART I

Selling in Today's Transparent World

CHAPTER 1

The Importance of You in Selling: Being a Real Part of the Solution

"Always be a first-rate version of yourself,
instead of a second-rate version of somebody else."
—Judy Garland

With today's marketers focusing the bulk of their resources on data, hype, and having a powerful online presence, you might think that salespeople are no longer relevant. You might fall into the trap of thinking that buyers don't need *people* in their buying process, taking up their time, when they can get "all the information they need" instantaneously over the Internet. Don't believe it! In today's world, where information is pervasive, *you,* the sales professional, are more important than ever.

What? The seller is more important than ever?

Yes, you heard me right. *You* are an essential component of what you sell. *You* are an essential component in many purchasing decisions.

YOUR ROLE IN THE SOLUTION YOU SELL

For more than a decade, "experts" have predicted the demise of the sales professional, arguing that online buying will significantly reduce or eliminate the need for salespeople. Yet I haven't seen that happen and I don't expect it will. What I have noticed, to the contrary, is that many online retailers are adapting how *they* sell to include chat features that offer site visitors the opportunity to connect with someone "live" to answer questions, discuss options, and clarify information. They have found that personal attention and assistance leads to selling more product.

This confirms my belief that there will always be a need for people to sell to people. In fact, as of 2010, the U.S. Bureau of Labor Statistics reports that there are over 13.4 million salespeople in the United States alone; and if you've checked the job listings lately, you'll find thousands of sales jobs waiting to be filled.

Why is that? Why do buyers still need salespeople when they have access to so much information? Let's take a closer look.

With the commoditization of many products and services, combined with the proliferation of information, *you* are often the differentiating factor in a prospect's decision to buy. While pricing, delivery, and the solution itself are important, what makes a buyer choose your solution over your competitor's is often you—your understanding of their situation, your concern for their need, your ideas about how they might best use your solution, and the confidence you give them in your company's solution. In short, they need what you personally bring to the sales process and solution during and after the sale—both in the business-to-business (B2B) sector, where solutions tend to be more complex, and in the business-to-consumer (B2C) marketplace, where personal experience and ability to relate to the consumer count—a lot. You add value to the solution and that value closes more sales.

Let me share an example from my own experience.

Early in my sales career, I took the advice of a mentor who suggested that I would win more business if I focused on my product, not my expertise, and modeled myself—style, dress, and demeanor—after a certain successful sales professional in my industry. Her message was that the product would sell itself if *I* didn't get in the way.

As a young upstart business owner, I thought I ought to listen. If that meant being invisible and just selling the product, well, that was okay by me. But that well-meaning, old-school coaching nearly cost me my first big sales opportunity—a multi-year training engagement in the financial services industry.

I managed to land the project after some quick scrambling, but it ended up costing me dearly—tens of thousands of dollars over a four-year period. Why? Because I was so busy trying to stay out of the way, so focused on the product pitch and being invisible, that I lost sight of the value *I* added to the solution, and, consequently, so did the client. Bottom line, I did a great job selling the *product* because they wanted my solution, but they didn't want me.

I salvaged the deal by hiring a trainer who had the experience the client requested and fit their suggested profile—someone older, preferably male, with gray hair or, better yet, bald!—while I took on the role of account executive. The percentage I paid my colleague deeply eroded my profitability and cost me referrals that went to him as the front man.

Over time, though, I gained confidence and began demonstrating my competence as a resource for the client, finding answers even when it wasn't my direct responsibility, driving the ongoing implementation, offering my experience and advice, and using my talents to "get it done."

After one particularly productive meeting where I was able to share some of my knowledge, insight, and suggestions, one of the leaders who had been part of the original selection team asked, "Where were *you* during the sales process?"

I wanted to stammer, "What? Where was *I*? I was the one working twelve-hour days to meet your deadlines and compile the information requested by your thirteen-person decision team, each and every step of the way." But I wisely kept my mouth shut as she went on to say that if the decision team had seen how smart, knowledgeable, funny, and personable I was, I wouldn't have needed to bring in my training colleague!

Hearing that hard truth was tough, but it taught me a valuable lesson about the importance of being part of what I sell—of letting my personality and unique strengths come through. If only I hadn't hidden behind the product, thinking that was all that mattered. If only I hadn't blindly followed my mentor's direction to focus only on the product and not incorporate "me" into the process and solution. If only I had demonstrated that *I* was part of the solution and the value they would receive, I would have closed the sale with fewer complications and a much higher profit.

FAKE IT 'TIL YOU MAKE IT: DOES THAT WORK?

What if you've been taught, or prefer, to focus your buyer solely on your product or service (solution)? What if you're not comfortable being a part of the solution—for whatever reason? Maybe you don't want to be seen as assertive or pushy, or you're feeling the pressure of not meeting quota; maybe you want to sell more and don't know how, or you've been "beaten up" by your buyers, by the market, by your manager, or by your competition. Maybe you are new to sales or in a new role, or have a new territory with different buyers, or have new solutions to sell. The reason doesn't matter much. The question is, can you "fake it 'til you make it" when it comes to confidence and competence, as many well-meaning managers, mentors, and colleagues advise when you're fighting through the fear, stress, and uncertainty that make up a day in the life of a salesperson?

I think not!

Perhaps it worked in the past, though I doubt it ever really did. It certainly doesn't work in today's world, where buyers have too many pressures on their time, resources, and attention to waste them on sellers who are disingenuous. And trust me, they can spot a fake a mile away—sellers who pretend to care, while they haven't taken the time to understand the buyer; sellers who lack knowledge, misrepresent the impact of their solution, or project uncertainty.

Buyers need sellers who really do care, who really do understand, who really can help them focus on the important information and discard all the rest. They need sellers who show up prepared to work with, and sometimes guide, them through the sales process effectively and efficiently.

But what if you genuinely lack confidence, or perhaps the necessary competence, to be the kind of seller buyers need today? You've come to the right place—the rest of this book will introduce you to the skills, tools, and techniques along with best practices and examples that will help you become a competent, valuable resource for your buyers, so you can approach any selling situation with genuine confidence.

THERE'S NOWHERE TO HIDE
IN A TRANSPARENT WORLD

If you're not yet convinced of the need to approach your sales with genuine competence and confidence, in today's transparent world your reputation, and that of your product and company, are more exposed than ever before.

For you as a seller, this transparency is a double-edged sword, opening opportunities to reach more buyers, to build stronger relationships and trust, and to differentiate yourself from the competition. At the same time, it leaves you and all you have ever done uncovered for your buyers and competition to view and analyze as well.

When buyers access the Internet or their network for information about your product and company, they look for reviews to learn of others' experiences, and frequently check up on the sales rep's "rep," too. One bad experience or questionable action can be broadcast instantly across the Internet, through social networks and consumer forum sites. And buyers pay attention. There's simply nowhere to hide and no room for faking it these days.

ADOPT AND ADAPT BEST PRACTICES
TO ESCALATE YOUR VALUE AND SALES

If it's important that you make yourself a part of your solution, and vital that you be "real," does that mean you should never model or borrow successful practices from top salespeople? No. This book is filled with best practices I hope you choose to adopt. The key, however, is to adopt *and adapt*—to make them your own.

Try them on for size, practice them, and make incremental adjustments to best fit your solution, your buyers, and the industry you work in. Make them genuinely yours by adapting them to fit your strengths, personality, skills, and expertise.

When you are "real" and a vital part of your solution, you give your buyers confidence, and you both experience new levels of satisfaction and success.

CHAPTER 2

Collaborative Selling: Where Every Conversation Matters and Everyone Wins

"I'm convinced that the world changes,
conversation by conversation."
—DANIEL PINK, **author**

Imagine this scenario. You're in a conversation, sitting across from another party—maybe one person, a couple, or a business team—with a wide desk or kitchen table between you. The surface between you is covered with documents, a computer, a telephone, and stacks of paperwork. Your prospective buyer is avoiding direct eye contact, afraid that you're there to *sell* them something or *tell* them something they have to do.

Now imagine a different scenario. You enter a conference room, office, or living room and your buyer smiles at you and greets you with a warm handshake. They invite you to sit next to them to share ideas and information. They are open when responding to your questions and engage with you collaboratively to discuss how you and your solution might help them, or provide something they want or need.

In which scenario do you have a better chance of succeeding? The second one, of course!

How do you make that happen? How do you create such a setting? You approach each sale using the collaborative selling approach you'll learn in this book.

WHY COLLABORATIVE SELLING WORKS

Buyers and sellers often approach a sales situation as if they are on opposing sides of the table—or opposite sides of a negotiation. That's what you saw in the first scenario.

Collaborative selling is about being on the same side, working side-by-side *with* your buyer to achieve something you both want. They want a solution; you want a sale. That's what you saw in the second scenario.

How then do you achieve what you both want? By focusing on the buyer.

When you focus on helping your buyer solve a problem, capture an opportunity, or get what they want or need, you give them greater value, build a trusting relationship, earn their loyalty, and end up with more sales. That's a situation where you both achieve what you want or need—short term and long term.

To help you remember the importance of focusing on your buyer throughout the selling process, I've developed an acronym—WiifT, pronounced "whiff-it" —which stands for "**W**hat's **i**n **i**t **f**or **T**hem?" Them is your buyer. It's spelled with a capital *T* because the focus is on *Them.*

The way you focus on the buyer is to make *their* problems, opportunities, wants, and needs the focus of *your* conversations and the reason for your solution. This leads us to another important acronym—POWNs, pronounced with the sound of the first *o* in *opportunity.* POWNs stands for **p**roblems, **o**pportunities, **w**ants, and **n**eeds—the items you work with your buyer to address or achieve. (I promise there are only three acronyms in this book for you to remember.)

Usually sellers are taught to find the buyer's want or need, and that is a great place to start. Yet when you look beyond the obvious want or need and help your buyer capture *opportunities* and solve *problems,* you gain their respect, earn their trust, give greater value, and create a stronger sense of urgency for adopting your solution.

These desired or not-yet-capitalized-upon opportunities and known and unknown problems are often the areas where you can provide the most value. In consumer sales, these may be life changers. Your solution may lead to less stress, healthier relationships, an improved quality of life, a more organized lifestyle or home, or a better work-life balance.

In corporate sales, they may be more complex, involve other departments, and help the company's customers or benefit the overall organization. Your solution might help them avoid future replacement costs or reduce maintenance expenses. You might help them realize a high-level benefit, such as eliminating redundancy with another department or improving the company's reputation. These are things your buyer may not have thought about, and yet addressing them benefits the buyer's company and puts the buyer in a favorable light within their own company.

When you think beyond immediate wants and needs, you make a huge difference to your buyer. The impact makes you more valuable than someone who just provides a product or service.

There are some misunderstandings about what collaboration is. There is a perception that collaboration is an arduous process, involving large teams of people and long timelines. Yet collaborative selling can be as simple as a single conversation, or a string of conversations, between a buyer and a seller—two-way conversations where the discovery and dialogue are part of the value the buyer receives.

In a nutshell, collaborative selling involves a buyer and seller, working together, conversation by conversation, to address the buyer's POWNs, with the outcome being that they both achieve something of value. The approach works whether your conversations take place face-to-face, over the phone, or through email.

COLLABORATION IS CONSULTATION PLUS

Consultative selling, which has been the norm for many years, positions you, the seller, as the expert in your field—the authority on your product or service. Your role has been to uncover your buyer's wants and needs, go off in a silo and develop a solution, and then return to explain how your solution matches the buyer's need. It's a "them and us" mindset, not a "working together" approach. Although the approach has been extremely effective for decades, it only addresses wants and needs, and misses opportunities and problems. Collaborative selling provides an opportunity to add much more value, as I'll explain later in this discussion.

Collaborative selling is also a more efficient sales process. Today's buyers are faced with more challenges than ever before. They are faced with what I call a "More and Less" syndrome:

Today's buyers face:

More	Less
Responsibility	Budget
Duties	Staff
Expectations	Time
Stress	Patience
Information	Decision-making authority

Sellers need an efficient, effective selling approach that doesn't waste their buyer's time or add to their "More and Less" challenges. You need to make every conversation count for your buyer, and that's what happens when you focus on WiifT. It's also what happens when your buyer becomes a part of the solution.

Remember the old saying that "two heads are better than one"? When you and the buyer bring your collective expertise and ideas together, you often come up with a solution that neither of you would have discovered alone.

A participant in one of my training sessions shared a situation where he was faced with a buyer's objection. Rather than trying to identify a solution to the objection by himself, he asked the buyer for their suggestion. The buyer's suggested solution was one the seller never would have thought of, leading the buyer to feel part of the solution and the seller to have a quicker decision with a committed buyer.

When you collaborate, your conversations are relevant for both you and the buyer, you reduce the buyer's fear or irritation of being "sold to" or "told to," better ideas are cultivated, and earlier buy-in is achieved, making the final sales decision much easier to secure. Sales close more quickly and both parties achieve their goals more efficiently, which is exactly what today's "More and Less" buyer needs.

WHEN YOU COLLABORATE, EVERYONE WINS

While we've established that collaborative selling focuses on the buyer and their POWNs, WiifT does not mean that the seller and the seller's company are unimportant. Instead, the winning solution or outcome benefits everyone involved.

In a traditional win-win situation, the goal is for two stakeholders—typically the buyer and the selling company—to win. With collaborative selling, the salesperson is also an important stakeholder.

I often hear sellers talk about feeling unimportant, caught between their company and their buyers. They express frustrations about being pushed to sell certain products, when they know a different solution will fit their buyer's POWNs better. This puts the seller in an uncomfortable situation where they can't possibly win. (By the way, if you find yourself in a situation like this, you can use the collaborative selling skills you'll learn throughout the pages of this book to also collaborate *within* your company to achieve a mutually beneficial result.)

When all parties work together, all the stakeholders win. It's a win-win-win or Win^3 (the "win-cubed").

Figure 2–1 graphically represents the Win^{3TM}, illustrating the interconnectivity of the stakeholders. The center components of the model are the means for accomplishing the triple win, Win^3.

Figure 2–1 Win^3 ™

How does each of these stakeholders win? Let's identify the possibilities when the sale is made and the buyer's POWNs are successfully addressed.

Your customer wins by having a solution to their POWNs. They may benefit in any number of ways, including more satisfaction in their work, less stress, more money or savings, more free time, peace of mind, an opportunity captured, an enhanced reputation, a problem resolved, a specific need or want fulfilled, and the ability to take on additional responsibilities and challenges.

Your company wins with increased revenue, additional sales, market share gains, customer retention, higher profit margins, higher employee retention, and a good reputation.

You, the seller, win by being gainfully employed and compensated, although that's not unique to the collaborative selling approach. What makes collaborative selling unique is that stronger buyer relationships and value are provided that create loyalty and lead to more, and often larger, future sales. You also become a valuable part of the solution, as we discussed in Chapter 1, and that builds greater confidence and satisfaction. Now we're talking Win^3!

What's more, the ripple effect of winning extends beyond the Win^3. There are additional stakeholders who also win. These include the buyer's company, your company's shareholders, others in your company who build the product and deliver the service you sell, or those who simply keep their jobs because your sales contribute to the company's bottom line. You can even add your personal stakeholders, including family and friends, because your well-being and financial success affect them, too. When a collaborative sale is made, and the buyer's POWNs are addressed, it's a string of wins all around.

About now you may be wondering, "Is it really possible for all the stakeholders to win?" It is possible when you focus on the components in the middle of the Win^3 model.

Conversation by Conversation, What Collaboration Looks Like

While collaborative selling might sound good in theory, it may be hard for you to picture how it really works. Let me illustrate with an example from my own experience.

We began at the table—the buyer and I—engaged in a relevant conversation about his business problems and opportunities and his training wants and needs. After a high-level review of our training solution, he was interested in learning more. What he wanted was to know the final implementation recommendation and costs—now!

I could have gone back to my office to devise the plan for him; instead, recognizing his personality type (more about that in Chapter 4), I decided to include him in the process right then and there. I asked if he wanted to build it with me.

Together we sketched out the implementation plan on a white board. I then added the investments while he observed and asked clarifying questions. He was able to see how each piece worked and how the costs were calculated. He was able to ask questions and get immediate responses.

The buyer was pleased, and yet I didn't get a *yes* that day. He wanted to finish his review of other vendors to determine if mine was indeed the best solution. Because we had built the solution together, I was confident that he wouldn't find a better fit.

It was a long thirty days before he confirmed that he wanted to work with me, and that our collaborative process was the deciding factor. After seeing how other training consultants worked, he recognized he didn't want his reps learning their techniques.

While not every selling situation requires the same level of collaboration, it was powerful in this case, and for this type of decision maker. If I had followed the typical path of taking in the information and then getting back to him later, I might not have earned his business, which I have now enjoyed for a productive—and profitable—ten years.

And just in case you think collaborative selling only applies in B2B sales, here's an example from a consumer sale. Kurt, a financial advisor, sat at the kitchen table with a couple discussing their retirement dreams, their plan for funding their children's education and weddings, and the vacation they wanted to take for their twenty-fifth anniversary.

Kurt asked questions of both the husband and wife for clarity, and facilitated the dialogue between them to prioritize. He then began to explain how he might help them achieve these financial goals. Kurt asked for their thoughts and feelings about various options, working with their existing financial investments and budget, and their needs for insurance. He helped them get in sync on their goals and their overall approach.

At the end of the conversation, Kurt made a commitment to put together a plan to achieve what they had discussed. Unlike what happened in my example, Kurt did go away to develop the plan; in this case it was necessary to develop the correct plan after researching options. At their next appointment, he illustrated the plan and connected it back to their goals and earlier discussion. He asked for their input, comments, and questions, and then asked if they were ready to move forward. They were.

HOW COLLABORATIVE SELLING WORKS
IN CHALLENGING SITUATIONS

At this point you may be thinking, "Those are great examples, except what about this situation—or that? What about the scenarios I find myself in? Does the collaborative selling approach always work?"

I'd like to respond with an absolute *yes*, but that would be naive, and I can't deny that there are some predicable situations where collaborative selling can be a particular challenge. What follows are some of the most common challenges you may encounter.

The Order-Dictating Buyer Challenge

While your intentions and approach may have evolved from "old school" selling, some buyers haven't made the switch yet. Some are conditioned, or trained, to expect you to simply take their order or dictate a solution. They either tell you what they want and expect you to find a way to get it to them, or they say "Tell me what you've got for me—oh, and make it inexpensive and fast!"

It can be tough to switch the focus from being an order-taking solution dictator to a collaborator. Still, it is possible. In these situations, try adjusting your approach and conversation to guide the buyer, including them in each step whenever possible.

I once worked with a VP of sales who told me he knew exactly what he wanted. He had done his research and had years of experience with solutions similar to mine. At first, he seemed like a dream come true. He came to me to fill a specific need. He had prequalified himself, done his research on me and my training services, and just wanted a price quote. In essence, he wanted me to be an order-taker.

Yet, in talking with him to get the specifics needed to develop the quote, I realized that what he was asking for would not get him the gains he wanted. I asked him if he was willing to consider additional information and options, allowing me to add my expertise, earn his trust, and educate him on a different solution to accomplish what he really needed.

He was adamant he didn't need a "consultant"; all he wanted was a price quote. I then explained that I might not be the right solution for him after all. I said I would not waste his time or money on implementing something that would not earn him the healthy ROI he needed. And, yes, I was willing to walk away if necessary. I knew I wouldn't have been successful in the long term following his solution, and the agony along the way was just not worth my time and energy.

The VP paused, and then agreed to give me an hour to discuss his situation further. What we discovered, together, was that we could build the right implementation plan. This "right-sizing" would provide him the outcome he needed and allow my team to make an impact for his team in a shorter time frame. The sale closed the next week.

The Misfit Buyer Challenge

When a buyer does not fit your solution—whether philosophically, in terms of budget, their timing, internal processes, or with their unwillingness to disclose necessary information—collaboration is going to be tough. I've had prospects who wanted me to help their sales teams learn how to coerce customers into action with hard closes, even when their buyers weren't ready. Others asked me to help their sellers pitch a solution, whether or not their buyer was qualified or interested. Neither request was in sync with my philosophy and approach. These were misfits for me and my solution.

When it's obvious that a potential buyer is not a fit, I've learned—the hard way, I assure you—that I will sell more if I move on to higher-probability prospects as early as possible.

For instance, I had a local buyer at a large retail store approach me about my sales training. The first several phone calls were stiff, and it was hard to get information from him. When he agreed to a face-to-face meeting, I thought we were making progress. The meeting was productive, until he asked me to put together a recommendation for several options.

Knowing that responding to his request would take between eight and ten hours of work, I knew I had to further qualify him to save both of us time. I explained that there were many options, and to ensure I didn't waste his time, I needed to identify the ones that fit within his budget. He was silent. I then asked, "What budget do you have for this initiative?" and he responded, "I'm not sure. I'll know the right number when I see it." Red flag! I again explained that I needed a range to work with, and he blurted out, "You aren't going to break me!"

Whoa! I wasn't trying to break him. This was relevant information that I needed to give him the most useful recommendation.

I knew that the likelihood of success with this buyer was slim, though I wasn't ready to call it a dead opportunity—yet. So I adjusted my efforts and produced a short-format recommendation with three options that addressed his questions and illustrated, at a high level, what we could do for him. It only took me one hour, instead of the many I would have put into a detailed proposal.

The result? He never responded to my fifteen follow-up inquiries over the next six months. I now qualify those buyers out early. If they aren't willing to discuss their budget and the viability of us working together, they aren't worth my time and effort.

If you think you're not in a position to walk away, look at what the most successful people do; they focus their time and energy on high-probability buyers. As one top performer told me, "When I learned the value of using the delete key, my business grew."

Procurement Buying Challenges

For those of you in corporate sales, the dreaded procurement sale can be another potential minefield. This is the corporate sale where you work collaboratively through the sales process with the end user or supposed decision maker, and then once the initial decision is made, the procurement team takes over.

What happens next? All the collaboration up to that point is ignored—now it's tough, old-school negotiating and getting beat up on price. The POWNs that had been addressed originally are no longer central to the final procurement decision.

Sound familiar? My company kept bumping into this kind of "vendor relations" with our larger clients. What did we do about it? We learned to collaborate with internal influencers and key decision makers. By assisting them in the sales process, equipping them to sell internally, and aiding them with any information or tools they need, we have ready-and-willing collaborators helping us navigate their internal procurement process.

This has worked so well for us, in fact, that we once had an internal collaborator tell us to prepare for procurement's demand to always secure a 10 percent discount. We were able to price our solution accordingly, and everybody won—a Win^3 was achieved.

The e-Relationship Challenge

Another complication in selling collaboratively is the buyer who wants or expects the "e-relationship." They prefer a "Send me this" or "Click on this link" approach to communication and the selling process.

While we should take advantage of electronic tools and technology to enhance the sales process, an e-relationship presents unique challenges when it's our main, or only, mode of communication. Instead of a two-way conversation with both parties engaged, we may end up with two streams of one-way communications and less opportunity to discover POWNs and motivations and thus more challenges in differentiating our solution from the competition.

I've worked with several buyers—and have existing clients—who prefer to handle most of our conversations through email. And I respect that, to a point. When we start to revisit questions and send virtually the same information back and forth, I rely on my three-back-and-forth guideline—that if we go back and forth three times on the same topic, I pick up the phone and call, or send an email saying, "Now that we've gone back and forth a few times with email, let's expedite the rest with a fifteen-minute phone call. What times work for you?" What's surprising is that often the answer is, "Call me now, I'm at my desk."

If the buyer is resistant, or the client prefers to maintain an e-relationship, I adapt my communication to include extra documentation and follow-up. I make sure my messages are short, including questions, specific examples, and relevant attachments.

One specific situation where the three-back-and-forth guideline doesn't always fit is when working with international buyers. Not only are there major time zone differences to work around, we may also have language differences that can best be bridged by communicating in writing. In these situations, ensure that your messages and information are supported with documentation, that they reference and recap earlier emails, and that clear action items and timelines are identified.

Time Pressure Challenges

Initial collaborative conversations can sometimes take a little longer than a "show up and throw up" sales call, and you may need to spend a little more time preparing to ensure that each conversation is productive and focused on WiifT.

If you're in a crank-out-the-calls sales environment, it may seem impossible to take the time for a collaborative approach. Yet I can assure you that many call centers have been able to adapt the systematic conversation framework we will cover in Chapter 3 to make their conversations efficient and value-focused. And if it does take a little longer on the first call, the information exchange early in the conversation shortens the selling cycle and saves time in the long run.

IS COLLABORATIVE SELLING WORTH THE EFFORT?

There are potential challenges with any approach to selling, and collaborative selling is no different. My belief is that as you read through the tips and strategies outlined in the remaining chapters, you'll decide that it's in your best interest to adopt and adapt these collaborative and WiifT-focused strategies. And, as a client recently reminded me, they are also in the best interest of the buyer.

These strategies may seem like extra work at first, and I won't say that collaborative selling is *easier*. What I have found, though, is that it's a matter of transferring energies and actions, rather than adding more; it's a matter of getting comfortable with the new techniques—and adapting them to make them your own.

If you believe that deep buyer relationships are important—relationships that lead to repeat business, referrals, and loyal customers—then you will find that the effort of collaborating is well worth it.

QUICK TIPS FOR COLLABORATIVE SELLING

- To keep your focus on the buyer throughout the selling process, remember the acronym—WiifT—which stands for "**W**hat's **i**n **i**t **f**or **T**hem?" Them is your buyer, spelled with a capital *T* because the focus is on *Them*.

- Keep a WiifT focus for each part of your selling process. This includes making *their* **p**roblems, **o**pportunities, **w**ants, and **n**eeds—POWNs, the items you work with your buyer to address or achieve—the focus of your conversations and the reason for your solution.

- Strive for a collaborative approach in your sales conversation by involving your buyer in connecting the solution to their POWNs; this will increase the probability of the triple win—Win³—for the stakeholders, which includes you, your buyer, and your company.

- Qualify the fit of your buyer early in the process. If the buyer is not willing to share information or is unable to give the time needed to your conversations, press the delete key or adjust the time and energy you have on higher-probability sales opportunities.

- For corporate procurement buying centers, use the commitment of your internal influencers and collaborators to navigate through the procurement process.

- To collaborate and involve your buyers as much as possible in e-relationship sales, focus on making your messages concise, include questions to involve Them, share specific examples, support information with documentation, reference and recap previous messages, and identify clear action items and timelines.

PART II

The What and How of Collaborative Sales Conversations

CHAPTER 3

Systematized Success:
Make Every Conversation Count

"Unless you try to do something beyond what you
have already mastered, you will never grow."
—RALPH WALDO EMERSON

Have you ever thought about the number of systems that are part of your day? Our nervous and digestive systems tend to our bodies. Man-made electrical systems power our televisions and coffeemakers. Accounting, manufacturing, and customer relations management (CRM) systems streamline our jobs. We approach almost every task we complete, from tying our shoes to operating a computer, in a systematic way.

Identifying the system—the organized or established procedure, arrangement, or pattern that leads to any outcome—helps us understand how things do what they do—from the earth rotating, to our body's need for food, to why a coffeemaker needs to be plugged into a working electrical outlet.

Systems are integral to our modern world and lives and they aren't new; the identification and study of systems dates back to Plato and Aristotle. No matter what you are doing, a system gives you consistency, reliability, repeatability, and confidence in the outcome.

A systematic approach to your sales conversations helps you more easily adopt the collaborative selling approach to build stronger sales results.

FIVE STEPS TO SYSTEMATIC SALES SUCCESS

How did you make your last sale? Can you specifically identify every action and step, the flow to your conversations, and what worked well? With a lot of thought you probably can track how you did what you did—from opening the conversation to closing and getting the "buy" decision.

This is because you are consciously or unconsciously using a system for your sales conversations. You already have established a routine and comfortable way of conducting yourself and your sales calls. Your routine has been adopted over the course of your career, and it's most likely very comfortable for you. You may even work through your sales conversations without a lot of thought about how you're doing it.

This routine is producing your current level of success. If you are satisfied with your results at this time, then you probably don't need the ideas and tools in this book.

But if you are like the top performers I know, you may wonder, "How do I sell even more?" and "How can I capture more sales, in less time, and with more ease?" Top performers look for incremental adjustments in their selling to help them sell more. This attitude of continual improvement is why I really enjoy working with top performers and willing students; they often discover that going back to the basics for their sales conversations can easily catapult their efforts and sales by 5 or 10 percent.

Or maybe you are newer to sales and trying to save time and shortcut the trial-and-error process to quickly ramp up your sales. In either case, one sure-fire way to become more proficient is to dissect how you work through your sales conversations to identify the system that leads you to success most often.

Such analysis is a lot of work and may be limited by time, your personal habits, and your experiences. Fortunately, you don't have to go to all the trouble of constructing a system that will lead to more sales conversation success. The five-step sales system I'm about to outline—WIIFT™—was developed by observing thousands of sales professionals around the globe and sharpened through application in many different industries.

I purposely use the acronym W-I-I-F-T (note all capital letters) for the steps of this system to give double meaning to the term WiifT (What's in it for Them) that you learned about in Chapter 2. WIIFT in all caps stands for each of the five steps—Wait, Initiate, Investigate, Facilitate, and Then Consolidate—in this guide to making every conversation count.

This system may challenge your current practices and actions. I ask that you put your assumptions, ego, and current beliefs on hold and objectively consider minor or major adjustments to your approach that just may elevate your sales in a short time.

The WIIFT sales system guides you toward a greater probability of success in every conversation, allowing you to:

- Ensure success with consistent and conscious actions.

- Replicate it over and over in all situations, with minor adjustments.

- Diagnose gaps in stalled sales or troublesome situations, allowing you to close the gap and advance the sale.

Your sales conversations gain efficiency when you take the related parts—introductions, POWNs analysis, building rapport and trust, negotiating, and closing sales—and organize them into a system.

Figure 3–1 WIIFT™

Figure 3–1 is your visual aid to the system that allows you to capture that Win^3 described in Chapter 2. Each component of the graphic represents a key principle to collaborative selling success:

1. *Prepare*, or preparation, is the foundation of your conversation and makes every aspect of your conversation more effective.

2. *Prove* is the umbrella over the whole system, present throughout the sales conversation and relationship. It begins in pre-sales and in every action you take or don't take for the entire sales cycle and relationship. Proving includes using information about your solution, company, and yourself.

3. The five steps of the system—**W**ait, **I**nitiate, **I**nvestigate, **F**acilitate, and **T**hen Consolidate (WIIFT)—are in the middle of the model as the center of your conversation success.

4. The dots are you! They indicate your involvement. Your expertise, credibility, and experiences are critical components in this equation.

We begin our overview of the model at the center, with WIIFT. As you read through this systematic approach to your conversations, think about your most successful sales conversations and how they have most likely followed these steps.

Step 1: Wait

Just as the first step of every system is the launch for the rest, your conversation success with WIIFT starts with the Wait step. *The purpose of Wait is for you to maximize the value of the time with your buyer as you prepare for the specific conversation on paper; a time when you break your preoccupation with everything else, and mentally begin to focus on this buyer and situation.*

This often is the step we miss because it's so easy to jump into a conversation without making the time to pull our thoughts or our words together when we have a sales opportunity. As a result, this could be the end of your sale instead of the beginning!

As the anchor to your conversation, this is the only step completely in your control. The Wait step is about preparation—which may begin days or even weeks before your initial conversation—with research, a review of prior documentation, or team meetings. It ends with your mental pause just before the actual contact with your buyer. When *you* are ready, move to the next step.

Step 2: Initiate

The purpose of the Initiate *step in WIIFT is to open the door to a value-filled conversation and connect with the buyer to build trust, engage them, and earn the right to ask questions.* This step begins your connection with the buyer. However, it does not only relate to a first-time conversation—it is applicable to the opening moments in every conversation.

Permission to talk business is earned by demonstrating your focus on *What's in it for Them?* from the very start. Initiate includes your greeting and introduction, confirms the reason for connecting and the time allotted for the conversation, then turns the focus directly to them. Even if you know the person, a good initiation makes a relevant connection to build upon. Initiating productively earns you the right to move forward to the third step.

Step 3: Investigate

From Initiate, your conversation easily flows into Investigate. *The* Investigate *step in WIIFT identifies the problems, opportunities, wants, and needs; qualifies the buyer; and clarifies the sense of urgency in addressing their POWNs.*

More than fact-finding for needs, although that is important, you expand your value and potential for collaboration by discovering and exploring problems, opportunities, and wants as well—the POWNs introduced in Chapter 2.

Collaborative sellers take a broader and more strategic approach to their sales conversations than just looking for their needs. They:

- Explore and review the current and future problems of their buyers.

- Aid their buyers in capturing opportunities for their business, roles, and lives that they might not have considered.

- Take time to explore the wants and emotional aspects of the buyer and situation. Even though most buyers make their business case or decision with logic, emotional factors are often the true underlying motivator to the decision.

Relevant open-ended questions asked during this step get the buyer talking while you actively listen, take notes, paraphrase, and ask additional questions. This lets you confirm that you both understand the buyer's

POWNs. The information gathered and discovered together, including whether this is a qualified buyer of your solution, opens the potential for collaborating in the next step.

Step 4: Facilitate

While the Investigate step is the crux for most consultative sales systems, collaborative conversations place at least as much emphasis on the Facilitate step. *The purpose of* Facilitate *is to make it easy to connect your solution to their POWNs and collaborate through objections or questions with Them.*

The key components of Facilitating are educating, recommending, and collaboratively exploring appropriate solutions for fit and value. Your customized recommendation to the buyer's POWNs presents only relevant information about features and benefits that apply to that person, situation, or company while generating a feedback loop with the buyer.

This collaboration also helps you constructively work through any concerns, questions, or objections: the basis for good negotiation. Matching the solution and working through objections leads the conversation into the final step.

Step 5: Then Consolidate

The "close" is often the target within a sales system. While we need to close the sale, focusing solely on the close can be limiting because not every sales conversation ends in a buying decision. In collaborative sales, *every* conversation should be consolidated and end with closure . . . for you and for them.

Then Consolidate is the last step of WIIFT. I took the liberty of using the letter "T" in "Then" to create a phrase that consolidates several key activities that close each conversation and eventually the sale. *The objective of* Then Consolidate *is to advance or make the sale by securing the decision* or commitment and clarifying the next steps. A commitment to a decision or action at the end of every conversation helps you advance the sale more quickly and eliminate redundancy in follow-up actions and conversations.

Consolidating or bringing closure begins with a recap of how your solution addresses their POWNs, then seeks a commitment to a decision and identifies the next steps for all parties.

Your success in securing a decision or commitment relies on the Investigate and Facilitate steps. The conversation does end with closure—a final confirmation of expectations and a sincere, personalized closing statement.

* * *

The WIIFT systematic approach to sales conversations is a road map for reaching a successful closure every time. Each step of WIIFT is useful on its own and also builds on the preceding one, making transitioning from step to step easy. As part of the system, each step can be dissected for study and application. You will realize greater and greater success as your skills become so habitual that the steps are connected seamlessly into a fluid, meaningful, and logical conversation with your buyer.

The WIIFT system isn't so specific and prescriptive that you become robotic in your conversations. It allows for flexibility for your style, industry, buyers, and situations. All of this allows you to be genuine, to be really *you*, as discussed in Chapter 1. Think of it as the curbs along the side of the road that keep us safe and guide us to our destination, yet leave room for us to maneuver within the lanes, even allowing for U-turns when necessary!

WIIFT is effective both in one-visit selling situations and for strategic sales. My consulting team follows the WIIFT system for the many steps in the corporate sales cycle that often occur over nine to eighteen months! This system is also used in three-minute telesales that are inbound. I wish I would've known about a systematic sales approach when I tried mall jewelry sales as a second job after college! Following WIIFT each time you are in conversation with your buyer, whether it is a three-minute or three-hour conversation, keeps the sale moving forward or lets you know that the probability is low and you can move your time and energy to more probable sales opportunities.

And now you've had your introductory overview of the five steps of WIIFT. Chapters 5 through 10 outline specific *whats* and *hows* for each step, sprinkled with plenty of examples and best practices. To keep yourself relevant, adjust the steps and tools to best fit your style, company processes, industry, and customer types.

WIIFT is the center of the model and is central to your conversation. However, the five steps are also surrounded by two actions that are just as important, Prepare and Prove.

PREPARE TO SUCCEED

Preparation *is the groundwork that makes every element of your sales conversation the best that it can be.* Preparation is critical. It's critical to each and every sale, especially in today's sales world, and it's critical for your long-term career. That is why Prepare is the *foundation* of the WIIFT system in Figure 3–1. Preparation *supports* the entire conversation. Though some sellers tell me that they do much better when they "wing it," I haven't observed that to be true—all sales pros benefit from the consistency, confidence, and greater efficiency of systematic preparation.

Preparation is a habit. The act of preparing is not difficult; it's a discipline. Preparation is physical in putting pen to paper or fingers to keyboard; it's also mental, as you will read in Chapter 5 on the Wait step.

As discussed in Chapter 1, *you* are central to the success of each sales conversation. I will make this point again and again throughout the book. You may get tired of reading it, but it's possibly the most important thing I have to say. Your input before and during the conversation significantly impacts the output or the results. The term "garbage in, garbage out" has stuck with me since I took computer programming classes in my MBA program. It's the same with your sales conversations—and if you do not *Prepare* with relevant, timely, intentional, and focused input, you can expect your output to reflect that.

When a seller from India adopted Preparation, he closed a $4.6 million sale in one visit. How? He gathered his team to spend time preparing for the meeting. They reviewed the buyer's Tribal Type (explained in Chapter 4), and adjusted their presentation order, talking points, and PowerPoint presentation to his Type. They practiced responding to the questions and concerns he might ask and built their confidence and competence for the meeting. Their preparation led to closing the sale in that single visit rather than in what would typically have been four visits for this type of opportunity. You can bet this man—and every member of his sales team—is a believer and vocal advocate of the power of preparation.

Preparation is so important I've included a tool and many tips and best practices in Chapters 5 and 12 to help you prepare efficiently and effectively.

PROVE THE VALUE

Prove *is the umbrella over the WIIFT steps, reminding us that we must consistently and systematically prove ourselves and the value of our solution in each conversation.* Proving your value and that of your solution is not a onetime occurrence; value is assessed by your buyer throughout the entire relationship.

Value is a subjective aspect of selling anything. Whether you have a tangible product or a service, the real value of what you are selling is determined by your buyer—not by you or your marketing department. You do, though, play a major role in proving value to the buyer. Your ability to provide the right proof at the right time reduces pricing concerns, profit margin erosion, and the objections you need to work through.

Your Personal Value

The value your buyer receives also is attached to *you*! The actual value your buyers will associate with the solution begins with their experience with *you*. While many sales professionals talk about quality and value as the responsibility of "corporate," product development, manufacturing, or marketing, every action you take, or don't take, provides value to your buyers or it doesn't.

For many years I represented a training solution in which quality was compromised because updates were released before they were ready and company leadership changed several times. During these transitions, many of my long-term clients told me the reason they continued to use the solution, despite its shortcomings, was because they wanted to work with me.

I didn't truly understand the implications of this until I developed my own sales training course. While I was confident that I could sell it into new companies, I underestimated the value my current clients placed on working with me and the impact that made in their willingness to adopt the new course for themselves. In the first year, I was pleasantly surprised when several clients told me that if I believed the new course was going to provide the skill and behavior-changing value they needed, they were "in."

One decision maker committed to implementing the new course with his international team without even seeing an outline of the materials. Another participated in an abbreviated preview of the course—her company's sourcing protocol demanded it—but she assured me that she knew in advance that she was going to say yes, because she knew that if she worked with me she would not have to worry or manage the process as tightly. She trusted me.

Only after both agreements were signed did I consider the ease in making the transition to the new course. Here was firsthand experience of the power of the personal value I had provided for years.

For your career, pause and reflect on the extra value *you* have added to your solution and for your buyer. Whether you know it or not, this personal value may have led to rewards you were unaware of.

Each week I hear powerful stories from sellers about the extra value they deliver, such as:

- A four-hour, last-minute drive to troubleshoot a row crop issue.

- Visiting customers at their homes instead of having them come to the office.

- Sending prepaid envelopes to make it easy to return documents.

- Connecting the customer to another solution for other POWNs.

- Physically walking them to a specific product location within a store.

These may not seem extraordinary, but they mean a lot to the customer. Don't underestimate the value you add to each sales conversation and to the buyer throughout the sales cycle.

Metrics Count in Proving Value

Though proof begins with you, it doesn't end there. You need to prove the value of your solution and your company throughout the sales conversation and the relationship as well.

Proving the value of your solution is essential at each stage of the sales process and cycle. Keep in mind that value is in the eye of the buyer and is more powerful when it is:

- Relevant to the person and the particular situation.

- Timely throughout the sales conversation and as current as possible.

- Specific with measurable data and detail if necessary. Even if the measures are anecdotal or qualitative, the more specific they are, the more they will resonate with the buyer.

Identifying and documenting metrics was far from a priority for me when I was a Human Resource Executive (back then we were called Personnel) at a bank. However, Bill Koeper, a mentor of mine for many years, helped me better grasp how metrics count!

Bill was the marketing and sales executive back when I still wanted nothing to do with the sales profession. He guided me toward measuring and documenting successes in HR so that I could sell my personal value when it came to performance review and bonus time with the president. I told him I thought that was self-serving. He told me it was smart business and good human relations. He explained that if I didn't keep track of my successes in a concrete way, the decision maker (in this case, the president) would not necessarily recall the value of what I had done all year.

Reluctantly, I agreed to begin this process of documenting value and I was pleasantly surprised with a larger bonus and salary increase that year. So I kept documenting for my own reference and used this proof of my value later in what was possibly one of the toughest sales challenges in my career.

My manager was a hard-driving, challenging taskmaster who determined much of the leadership team's worth on face time in the office. He even randomly called our desks on Saturday mornings to see if we were putting in extra time.

Years later, when I wanted to work part time to spend more time with my growing family, you can imagine the likelihood of a win for me. This was the early 1990s, before professionals were given reduced work schedule or flextime options. My colleagues doubted I'd get approval, but Bill thought I could. With his guidance I developed a recommendation that incorporated my documented value from the previous two years. And it worked! I got the deal to work three days a week *and* to add a lower-salaried person to my staff to take on some of my responsibilities.

It was a personal win that I am still grateful for to this day. Not only was I spending more time with my children, something I can never replace,

I was also able to care for my terminally ill mother. I closed a nontraditional sale that was a Win[3] for my family, for me, and for the company.

Providing proof isn't a "once-and-done" step. Too often I have seen sellers and sales teams provide great value, deliver their solution, and then move right on to a new solution with that customer. Whoa! They miss a great opportunity to review with the customer how the delivered solution tied into his or her POWNs and the benefit or value it provided.

Whether proving the value of our own personal efforts to internal personnel or to buyers, specific measurement is memorable and provides substance to the proof. Before you connect with any buyers, take the time to identify the value they will receive from you, your solution, and company. Maintain a list of data, testimonials, and successes that you can use throughout your relationship.

＊　＊　＊

A productive sales conversation is more probable when you follow the WIIFT system steps, and support your conversations with proper Preparation and Proof. The next section of this book provides further details on the five steps of WIIFT, as well as tips and tools to further systematize your conversations and make every conversation count.

QUICK TIPS FOR USING THE WIIFT SYSTEM™

- Follow the *WIIFT* five-step sales system—**W**ait, **I**nitiate, **I**nvestigate, **F**acilitate, and **T**hen Consolidate—to make each of your conversations the most productive.

- Focus on *WiifT* (What's in it for *Them*?) through each step to move you forward to the next step of your conversation predictably and logically.

- *Prepare* for conversation success. Make the time to identify the objective of your conversation and how you will make the conversation about Them, not you or your solution. Proper preparation for the conversation ensures it is value-filled for you and Them. Your gains are efficiency, consistency, and closed sales.

- *Prove* yourself and your solution. Provide relevant, substantive documentation throughout your conversation and relationship with the prospect.

CHAPTER 4

Tribal Types: Work and Sell with Buyers the Way They Want to Be Worked With

"Dealing with people is probably the biggest problem you face,
especially if you are in business. Yes, and that is also true
if you are a housewife, architect or engineer."
—DALE CARNEGIE

People are complex. What works well for your approach, word choices, and pace in one conversation may implode in another. Some people need to know every option and piece of information and will describe ideas and stories in every nitty-gritty detail; some have no real interest in you as a person, their interest is only in what you can do for them. Still others want to be your new best friend and the business at hand or important decisions can wait. And then there are those people who seem to need assurance and supporting data before they will do or decide anything.

As discussed in Chapter 3, using a system yields many benefits, but a system that involves people also presents unique challenges! Though the WIIFT sales system is easily learned, its implementation for each conversation is significantly impacted by the person in the conversation with you.

That's why the WIIFT system, a people system, needs to be adjusted for each individual and situation.

It can be frustrating figuring out how to get people what they need or want in each conversation. Having a model to assist you in understanding the different types of people is extremely valuable. Using models to understand people's unique behaviors or personalities is not a new concept; there are many models that describe individuals' unique characteristics.

In sales and service roles, where meeting dozens of people in one day is the norm, it's not easy to identify and use many of the models and assessment information immediately during a conversation. Having an "in the moment" tool to identify and adapt to the working style and communication preferences of others is most helpful.

INTRODUCING THE TRIBAL TYPES™ MODEL

The Tribal Types model is designed for one specific purpose: to help you identify a buyer's "type" and then adapt how you work and sell with that particular person *in the moment.* Why "tribal"? The name originated when I was traveling in Brazil for work with Motorola in 2008. My travel guide shared a different perspective for describing groups of people—*tribes.* He explained that the Copacabana beach scene in Rio de Janeiro is full of different tribes, or groups of people—teenagers, families, and singles—with similar customs who congregate in specific areas each weekend. Their shared customs include communication styles and preferences and so much more!

The word "custom" is important to understanding Tribal Types. A custom is an established practice, action, or thought process used by someone or a group of people. Customs are not only about what is innate or natural to people. They are practices that have been learned and adopted. When we work with others, their natural tendencies and preferences do matter. Yet we need to also take into consideration the environment they work in and their past experiences, as they contribute to their current practices, habits, and needs—their customs.

On my return to the United States I built upon my knowledge of personality and preference models by adding the customs component, and designed the Tribal Types model. This model is the end result: an "in the moment" tool to easily identify customs and characteristics so you can quickly adapt how you work with individuals through the buying process and in each conversation throughout your relationship.

To make the Tribal Types model easy to remember and, more important, easy to use, I have identified four distinct types. Yes, people *are* much more complex than four categories can explain, but with these four types as a guide, you are well equipped to make the necessary adjustments to work effectively with most people.

This chapter introduces the four Tribal Types—*Achievers, Commanders, Reflectors,* and *Expressers*—followed by specific information on how to identify each Type as well as strategies for selling and collaborating with them.

Additional information and how-to's for working through each step of the WIIFT sales system with the Tribal Types will be included in Chapters 5 through 10.

Figure 4–1 Tribal Types™

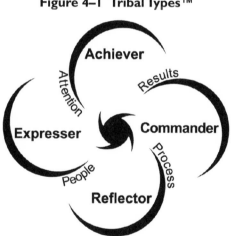

The Tribal Types model, Figure 4–1, illustrates several important points:

- The Types overlap in customs and behaviors and are therefore displayed in open arcs rather than closed circles or boxes.

- The words that begin on the tip of the inner arcs identify a key focus for the Types on either side. For instance, a focus on Results is associated with both the Achiever and Commander types.

• The middle of the model—the revolving center—is the *neutral zone.* From this center, you are able to switch directions and quickly move to the applicable Tribal Type customs. The neutral zone is often the safest place to begin because from there you can adjust your words, pace, and focus to the person and situation.

Using Figure 4–1 as your guide, read the descriptions of the four Tribal Types that follow. Look for the patterns of customs in people you know and have worked with. You'll be able to easily identify people you know in the different Tribes.

ACHIEVERS

Achievers are generally easy to pick out. They are high energy, quick, impulsive, and always on the move. They can be abrupt, confident, independent, impatient, and are often fast talkers. It is not uncommon to see (or feel) their energy as they are often tapping a foot or jiggling their legs.

Achievers' work spaces may appear cluttered and messy, but they can usually find what they need. They can seem dominating in their actions and conversations in their quest to get things done.

Working Style

When working with Achievers, you will notice they have many goals and priorities and they talk about their past achievements. Often they give tight deadlines and short timelines for getting things done. Because they work quickly, they assume others must as well. A change in plans isn't usually too bothersome for Achievers, as they change their priorities often.

Achievers will slow down if there's a good reason, but it can be hard for them to stop suddenly when they are in motion. I compare this to a fast-moving train. The train moves quickly, and when there is an obstacle or reason it needs to stop, it takes a while to slow the momentum in order to change direction or come to a halt. Achievers are generally open to other ideas, but if you catch them in mid-motion, it may take a while for them to hear you or notice that there is a benefit to doing something a different way.

Achievers want credit for what they accomplish. Their independent and confident nature may make it seem as if acknowledgment for their work doesn't matter, but it does. Some may like public displays, but many do not. What is important is that their achievements are documented. Often they will have trophies and certificates displayed somewhere in their workspace.

Word Choices The language clues you will hear from Achievers include "effectiveness," "efficiency," "results," "time," and "quick." They will use more "I think this" statements than "What do you think?" questions. They will talk about results, achievements, getting an answer, and asking for the bottom line. Achievers like to "tell it like it is," and while this candidness is helpful, it can also be seen as abrasive.

Level of Detail The level of detail important to Achievers is often low. They will grasp an idea or concept quickly and at a high level and be ready to move forward. The movement might be premature, but they like things to keep moving. They do not prefer to deal with details and have been known to skip steps or details to reach an end result more quickly.

Fears Common fears for Achievers include loss of respect, wasted time, loss of power, or being behind.

Value That Achievers Want from You

Achievers find value in someone who can help them get things done quickly, preserve their time, produce results, provide a lack of distractions, give them the opportunity to be first or to try something new, and provide high-profile connections. Though often they tell you what they want from you, they appreciate someone who is strong enough to clarify options or to push back to make something even better or quicker.

COMMANDERS

Commanders are reserved and controlled in their speech and body language. They may fold their arms across their chest and they often make direct eye contact. They are planners—precise, orderly, serious, and methodical.

Commanders' work spaces and homes are extremely organized. Their folders and filing systems are set up logically for the way they work. "Everything in its place" may be their motto. They tend to be conservative dressers and use more formal language. They are practical, diligent, persistent, and like to solve problems.

Working Style

Commanders are analytical, logical, and systematic, and their decisions are data-driven. They are planners and can be critical of others' plans or lack thereof. Commanders do not need a lot of social interaction within the work day and often run very agenda-driven meetings. Commanders generally do not appreciate a lot of small talk in meetings. This does not mean they are not interested in others. They just prefer to get to the agenda and if there is time at the end, often will engage in more personal conversation.

They are competitive and like to win with their ideas and actions. Taken to the extreme, they can be seen as bureaucratic.

Commanders are usually very prompt and become irritated when others are not. They will ask for calendar invitations, pay very close attention to details, and want specifics for any requests for information and deadlines. They may bog down decisions with analysis and strive for accuracy, and they will spend the time needed to "get it done right."

Word Choices Commanders' language is more formal and includes thinking words such as "why," "review," "compare," "validity," "analyze," "logic," and "control." Common phrases include, "How do you know?" "What proof is there to support that idea?" "What's the primary source?" "Research shows," and "Is that an opinion or suggestion?"

Level of Detail Commanders prefer and use a high level of detail. They are the people who will find the typos in your materials and point them out to you. They will review details over and over and want to know how information was calculated, determined, or secured. The accuracy of the data is as important as the depth and quantity.

Fears Common fears for Commanders include missing something, being wrong, losing, being criticized, and dealing with emotions—anyone's emotions: theirs, their colleagues, or yours.

Value That Commanders Want from You

Commanders know what they want. They generally have completed their own research, and their first questions to you may be about your knowledge. They will often test sellers at the beginning of a relationship to ensure they can trust their information and proposed solutions.

Commanders look for a seller who is accurate and can help them be right. They want substance and an organized approach to the sale, relationship, and solution. Commanders want to be involved in all decisions related to their situation, and their ideas and opinions need to be acknowledged. They like options with detailed pros and cons presented to them for analysis.

REFLECTORS

Reflectors are cooperative, friendly, patient, agreeable, good listeners, and people-focused. Although they do not show a lot of energy, that doesn't mean they don't have it. It simply means they will appear more reserved than others and will not seek attention in a crowd.

Often they stand on the fringe in group situations to observe the dynamics, situation, and people before contributing. When you ask a Reflector a question, they will pause for what may seem like a long time before responding. They prefer to think their answer through before stating it out loud.

Often, Reflectors will be softer talkers, not because they are meek, but because they do not see a need to call attention to themselves. You will find that Reflectors enjoy being a part of a team, if the team is cohesive and people carry their weight.

I've often seen Reflectors become frustrated because their opinion isn't asked or they aren't asked to participate in high-profile activities. The reason they do not raise their hand first is not that they are less interested, but that they want to think before volunteering.

Working Style

You will find that Reflectors are careful in their approach to their work. They may ask a lot of questions before agreeing to or beginning new activities. They are not your first adopters for ideas or productions. They are process-focused; if there is a policy or procedure, they will follow it and find any holes in it. Reflectors don't like any steps to be missed or skipped.

Reflectors are precise and thorough. There is no rushing them; the stress of pressure may even slow them down and surely frustrate them. In work meetings, Reflectors often will not be the first to express a new idea or to volunteer information. They will wait for their opinion to be asked. If it isn't, they may show annoyance later or say "Well, no one ever asked me."

Word Choices You will hear Reflectors use words such as "how," "feel," and "process," and questions and phrases such as "When should…?" "This is how we do it," "Don't want to rush through this," "Are you sure?" "Who else?" and "Has that worked before?" They are diplomatic in their speech and careful with their word choices. When taken to the extreme, this can be perceived as weak or wimpy, though it isn't.

Level of Detail Reflectors pay attention to details. They prefer a high level of detail and are able to recall details or know where to get the data if needed. They will create reference information for themselves and for everyone else to document the process and keep everyone following it.

Fears Common fears for Reflectors include missing something, the unknown, change, breaking the rules, loss of security, and instability.

Value That Reflectors Want from You

Reflectors value a logical and consistent approach to situations. They like information in advance and want to know the steps involved. They appreciate someone helping them through the decision-making process by providing all the information they need and not pressing them. They do appreciate a timeline for a decision to be made as it helps them finalize the decision. Reflectors value good listeners because they are good listeners.

EXPRESSERS

Expressers are energetic, social, and talkative. They will work the room and talk to many people. They may appear to be disorganized and indecisive. They talk a lot about personal things and want to know how you feel. Expressers seem to know everyone, or at least they want to, and networking is important to them. Their emotions are often very visible; some might even say they wear their heart on their sleeve.

Expressers tend to be trendy dressers and don't mind clothes that call attention to themselves; they are the people wearing holiday ties and scarves! They are animated talkers and use their body language to add color and content to their verbal message. You may notice they use smiley faces in their written messages.

Working Style

Expressers are people-focused and prefer a consensus for activities, decisions, and work flow. Their decisions are swayed heavily by the impact the outcome will have on others. Sometimes, Expressers come off as a little scattered to other Types because they want to explore and discuss all ideas and check in with everyone involved.

They may work outside the established systems or processes to get things done through their connections. They are demonstrative in their appreciation for others and appreciate recognition for who they are and their contributions to the team.

Expressers are supportive of everyone on the team and may implement new ideas or start many activities and then lose interest before they are completed.

Word Choice Expressers use stories and lots of words in describing something or responding to a question. They will start many discussions with "Who?" Other words you hear Expressers use include "awesome," "like," and "happy." Phrases include "that's great" and "I feel" and often include questions such as "How are you?" "Do you like this?" and "What do others say?" The information they provide is not always given in a straightforward, linear path, and in its extreme this may make the Expresser appear disorganized.

Level of Detail Expressers have a lower attention to detail than the other Types and prefer to be visionary and big picture–focused. They will not read or research pages and pages of information.

Fears Common fears for Expressers include not being "in," being seen as unimportant or insignificant, rejection, disappointing others, and not being valued as a person.

Value That Expressers Want from You

Expressers want to like their seller. They find value in sellers they can connect with and who can help them navigate the decision-making process. They appreciate the opportunity to be first or be able to introduce something new to others. They are often first adopters of an idea if they like the people involved. They want loyalty and need to know that they are cared for as a person, not just as your buyer.

IDENTIFYING AND USING TRIBAL TYPES

After introducing the Tribal Types model to sellers, I've heard some say, "I guess I can *act* like I'm _____." You can fill in the blank with "interested in them," "just like them," or "caring." Acting is *not* the intention of a Types model. The model is to help us:

- Understand that not everyone is like us.

- Identify different ways people communicate and work and the value they need from us as sales professionals.

- Speak *their* language and adapt, acknowledge, and appreciate *their* customs.

To use the Tribal Types information in the first part of this chapter effectively, first identify your own Tribal Types. This awareness allows you to determine how you normally operate and communicate. Why is that important? Because most of the time we operate in the way that is most natural and comfortable for us.

As the president of a small company he was introduced to the model said, "If I assume that 25 percent of the population falls into each of these four Tribal Types, this means that for forty-eight years I have potentially been working and communicating with people incorrectly 75 percent of the time."

What an observation! How true this may be for many sellers. If you are consistent in your own selling style, working style, conversations, pace, and level of detail, you may be miscommunicating and working with people less effectively than you could be 75 percent of the time!

The Tribal Types identifiers and tips will help you to determine the necessary adjustments you can make so your conversations count to each buyer. These adjustments will vary by person and situation.

You may need to slow down your approach, provide more or less detail, be more open to personal connections, or prepare more substance or facts. This does not mean you need to change who you are. Instead, adapt the way you are working and communicating with your customers and prospects to make the experience most relevant and comfortable for them.

Use the simple Tribal Types Tool on page 196 of Chapter 12 for identifying the four types. Begin using the Tool to identify *your* preferred customs; do not prejudge your Type. Their practice on colleagues, your spouse or partner, and friends. The more you use this tool, the easier it will be to identify adjustments you can quickly make to sell and collaborate more easily with your buyers.

Look for the Customs Clues

To identify any individual's Tribal Type, observe all the clues they provide. The clues can be visual or audible. If your conversations are telephone-based, pay close attention to the audible nuances such as pace, word choice, tone, and level of detail they use. It is amazing what clues are present when you look and listen for them.

In written correspondence, notice who uses full sentences and a greeting and who does not. Ever get an email where the whole message is typed in the subject line? Often that's the sign of Achievers, who think they are saving time.

A while back, I was supposed to call a prospect and replied to her email with a request for her phone number. She replied, "It's in the Subject line." I missed that detail because the way my screen displays messages (I would have had to scroll over to the right to see it, and that's not something I typically do). This little email was a strong indication that I would be dealing with an Achiever, and gave me insight as to how this individual works: quickly and without a lot of details.

In written correspondence, notice that some people are friendlier with a sentence or two of small talk at the beginning of their email message. This is a clue for you to engage with them in the same way in your return email.

It does take effort and energy to make the adjustments for the different Tribal Types—especially if they are the opposite of you. Over the longer term, I've observed that most buyers will begin to blend their customs with yours so that you are working together in a way that is most comfortable for both of you. But beware, under stress or time pressure they will quickly revert to their preferred customs and you need to be ready to adapt.

So, where do you start in your conversations and relationships? The neutral zone at the center of this model. It's the place where we should work from most often. Being neutral allows you to quickly switch directions to make the adaptation necessary "in the moment."

TIMELY TIP

You will find that people pick up customs from their work role and environment. They adapt their communication and working behaviors to be successful. As your conversations continue with them, you may find their actual preferred customs are different than your first impression of them. That is why the neutral zone is the safest place to begin *each* conversation. From there, you can quickly adapt to the customs that are important to them at that time.

STRATEGIES FOR SELLING WITH TRIBAL TYPES

Knowing Tribal Types has accounted for more closed sales and stronger relationships than I can possibly mention here. My participants regularly report successes they attribute to their identification of and adjustments for Tribal Types.

A seller from the medical device industry sent me this note:

"By identifying [that the prospect] was a Reflector, I gave more time to the investigation and asked her something I never normally ask to explore the risks of not doing something, 'What would happen if . . . ?' She took a few moments and responded, and then opened up about some of her concerns with what was currently going on in her facility. This openness and additional information allowed me to talk with her about how our product would help—and set the stage to advance the sale."

He then shared that she had scheduled a meeting with the entire Board of Directors the following week.

From the experiences of my workshop participants, as well as my own, the following selling strategies will help you increase your sales opportunities with each of the Tribal Types.

Achievers

Achievers appreciate a seller who helps them get things done in an uncomplicated and efficient way. Strategies for selling and working with Achievers include:

- *Use bullet points in writing and be clear—and succinct—in your speech.* Achievers don't want to be bogged down with a ton of information or extra words. They value you "netnetting" ideas, suggestions, and questions.

- *Be prepared to move to the next step quickly.* Have necessary papers and next-step information with you or available, but don't bring it out or complicate the conversation unless the information is needed for a specific reference. Achievers don't want extra stuff or information. Be ready to provide it when they ask or need it.

- *Ask about time.* Find out how much of it they have allotted for your conversation. Even if you have scheduled thirty or sixty minutes, you may find them hoping it will only take half that amount of time. While some say it's dangerous to give Achievers an option on time, if you don't that doesn't mean their concern goes away; they may be more distracted not knowing how long they will be with you.

- *Adjust to their pace.* This does not mean you have to rush. It means you have to identify what is necessary and what is not. Often you will need to help Achievers slow down a bit to cover what is needed. They may find this frustrating. Your ability to explain why they need to slow down or back up or explain What's in it for Them is critical to getting their time and attention.

- *Explain your intent or why specific details will be important to them.* It may seem logical to skip details with Achievers and while it is important to reduce and take care of details for them, such as completing paperwork or reducing the number of options they should consider, don't skip what you know is necessary information. Use results and outcomes when describing benefits. Words like "efficiency," "results," and "effectiveness" are powerful Achiever words.

- *Compliment Achievers for their accomplishments.* Acknowledging a success of theirs or asking about one often gets them talking as much as Expressers.

- *Meet all deadlines.* The old "underpromise and overdeliver" mantra is helpful. However, note that if you accomplish something in a shorter period of time than you committed to, that shorter time frame will be their new expectation of you going forward.

- *Don't waste Achievers' time.* Be brief, get to the point quickly, and be decisive. Stay on topic and don't be insulted if Achievers abruptly cut you off to move things along.

- *Provide only the most viable choices for Achievers to select from.* This allows them to "net" out their options quickly. They don't want a long document or list of all the options; they value that you limit the options to their best choices.

A long-term client of mine, Farrell Riley-Sileno, is an Achiever. She prefers to give me direction, is always short on time, wants her information as succinct as possible, and is not often looking for small talk or a personal connection. She values my assistance in accomplishing her objectives and goals. A recent conversation with her reminded me of all of these traits when after thirteen minutes of reviewing her strategy, she asked me to send her information in a specific format and then said, "Okay, you know me, no time to chitchat, send me that information, buh-bye." Had this been someone I did not know well, I might have been insulted, but knowing her as I do, I wasn't the slightest bit offended.

Commanders

Commanders find value with a seller who helps them in a logical and organized way. Strategies for selling and working with Commanders include:

- *Prepare a coherent and concise conversation with supporting information and agenda.* Ask for a Commander's input on the agenda either before the conversation or at the very beginning of the conversation.

- *Stick to the agenda unless you ask for permission to deter from it.* Commanders may want to put your new idea or information on hold until they get through what they want to discuss.

- *Have more information and details in writing as backup;* supporting data is always good! Commanders will analyze all information so be prepared to show them the proof behind the data if you are questioned. They value primary source documentation.

- *Don't be overly friendly at first.* Commanders are not people to hug or double handshake. A firm and formal approach works best.

- *Keep your conversations work- or agenda-focused at the start and follow their lead in the level of personal talk.* I have found that with Commanders, you know you have made a good connection when they initiate small talk or personal conversation at the end of the meeting.

- *Set realistic deadlines.* Ask Commanders for the realistic time frame and confirm deadlines before ending your conversation.

- *Don't work from your opinion or gut instinct.* Make sure your actions and decisions are based on facts, not theory or speculation.

- *If there is a problem or objection, ask for Commanders' help.* They can assist you in identifying how to work through it.

- *Follow up your conversations with a short written summary and confirmation of next steps.* Include time frames.

Early into my corporate sales career, I ran into a challenge with a Commander. When I first met him, after two easy and fantastic conversations with an Expresser manager on his team, he directed me to my seat in the conference room—directly across the table from him.

He told me what the agenda was and in what order he wanted information from me. He shared specific details on his needs and what he thought he needed in a sales training solution. At one point he even reached across the table and took my note pad to review the notes I had been writing. Thankfully, he concluded I had taken accurate notes.

The next step was a presentation to his management team. It went so well, he suspected that I was manipulating them in some way. The other managers remained positive though, and he kept moving forward in the buying process.

Further in the sales process, I was not reading his signals that it was time to ask him for a decision, and he finally said, "Nancy, I'm going to do your job for you; we are ready to implement this training."

Fortunately, despite the rough start, I delivered what was promised, kept this individual's needs in mind as we worked with his team and provided factual updates each week, and even learned more about him as a person. I must have done something right, because when he moved to a new company, he sought ways to use my services there as well.

Reflectors

Reflectors appreciate a seller who guides and supports their efforts without overt pressure. Strategies for selling and working with Reflectors include:

- *Talk at a normal pace.* Don't talk down to Reflectors or so slowly that they feel you think they are mentally slow.

- *When asking questions, share your intent and context before the question.* Then pause for up to twenty seconds while they first mentally process their response—and listen. Don't rush their answers. It will be worth the wait! As they respond, don't interrupt; let them complete their sentences and thoughts. Never try to finish a thought for a Reflector.

- *Ask questions and share opinions without being too aggressive.* Though Reflectors need assistance and some assertiveness, do not be too pushy or demanding on time and final decisions. Plan enough time in your conversations to review details, answer detailed questions, and allow Reflectors to explore options.

* *Assist Reflectors in making a decision by asking for deadlines that are reasonable.* Ask how much time they need to examine the information, and offer your assistance in reviewing options and details. If they ask for more time than you feel is needed, ask if there is any way it could be done to fit a shorter timeline.

* *Provide an agenda and questions to review in advance of your conversation.* Reflectors will take the time to review and prepare their responses. This will save time during your conversation and provide more thorough information.

* *Give attention to Reflectors for who they are and the value they provide.* Make an effort at the beginning of your conversation to connect with them personally before jumping into your agenda. Once they know about you and that they can trust you, it will alleviate any fears or concerns they have. It also answers any questions they may have about you before you get started and will help them be more open during your conversation.

* *Share specifics and details about how your solution works and the process you will work through with them.* Let Reflectors know exactly what happens after they make a decision.

* *Give Reflectors opportunities to meet others on your team when possible.* This provides a sense of security and knowledge of a backup if you aren't available.

* *Encourage Reflectors to make suggestions and share their opinions, not just facts.* They are generally observant and may have an idea no else would have thought of. Often this information will not be volunteered unless it is asked for.

I have had the privilege of working with Laura Erickson for over a year. Laura is a Reflector. Laura appreciates that I give her information in advance of our planning calls. She is always prepared and likes to collaborate and talk through ideas before we commit to them.

Laura's follow-up information is also precise and well thought out. As a manager, she is very good with tracking details and setting specific expectations. She appreciates the additional conversations we have that relate to her in more than just her sales role.

I have found that when I wait and let Laura process her ideas or responses without interrupting, the information is always very valuable.

Expressers

Expressers appreciate a seller who treats them well, provides personal attention, and helps them stay on track. Strategies for selling and working with Expressers include:

- *Plan to spend more time in a conversation with an Expresser.* This will allow for personal connections, stories, and tangents.

- *Be more direct than with other types to keep the conversation focused.* By sharing intent and context with Expressers before the question you aid them in focusing their response to relevant information.

- *If an Expresser's response is getting too long, it is okay to interrupt and redirect them.* Apologize for cutting them off and then ask a new question or redirect as necessary.

- *Pay attention to Expressers and offer genuine compliments, credit, and recognition.* Don't dominate the conversation.

- *Ask Expressers for their ideas, opinions, or suggestions.* Then prepare to listen as they will have a lot of them. Listen closely, as there are often good nuggets to be mined from the information.

- *Remember special dates and events such as birthdays, work anniversaries, where they were on vacation, etc.* This personal touch is especially important to Expressers.

- *Take careful notes to document information and action items.* Take care of as many details as possible since Expressers will not naturally keep track of details and you don't want the details missed. Send a short, written follow-up with a summary of the details, commitments, and actions. Include a note on how happy you were to spend time with them and what you specifically appreciate about your conversation or them. Be prepared to follow up with them more than once.

• *Invite others to the conversation if final decisions need to be made to allow Expressers to get the consensus they prefer.* Ask permission from the Expresser first though so he or she doesn't feel you are going over their head or lessening their importance.

• *When explaining your solution, use stories and anecdotes that are people-focused.*

I have had the privilege of working with many high-energy Expressers in my business. Kristine Amara and I connected on the very first phone call—a referral. By the second phone call, she was already my internal influencer to navigate the complex strategic decision process in a large company.

Because of Kristine's ability to understand the people in each role, we were able to position the sales training for each decision maker's needs. She had balanced her Expresser customs and was able to take care of the details and to deliver on what was promised.

My association with Kristine was important and we enjoyed a fantastic five-year working relationship providing great value to those on her team. Keeping her in mind, as a person, was just as important to my success as was the "real work" done. She was an advocate of me and my solution over and over again.

* * *

Did you recognize yourself and others you work with as you read through the discussion of Tribal Types? When we pay attention there are clues we will find. There are many ways to collect information about a person's customs, traits, and habits if you observe the signs and clues they provide about what is important to them, how they want to work, and their preferences for communication. The value of the Tribal Types tool becomes evident when you use the information to communicate more effectively "in the moment."

One very final comment about Tribal Types: People are, as I said at the beginning of the chapter, much more complex than can be described in these four Types. You will find that some people are a delightful—or not so delightful—combination of several Types. The more you pay attention to the customs, the more you will notice unique combinations and the easier it will be to make the adjustments that matter for that person.

QUICK TIPS FOR USING TRIBAL TYPES

- Identify your own Tribal Type first. Acknowledge how you prefer to work and communicate. This awareness will allow you to adjust as necessary from your normal actions when dealing with other types.

- Use the neutral zone. Top sellers seem like chameleons because they easily adapt and work with different people in different ways. The neutral zone provides you a safe place to quickly identify clues of how to work and communicate during each conversation. From there, adjust to the pace, language, and focus on value that is relevant to the Tribal Type.

- Remain flexible with your approach in each conversation. Don't judge or box in your contacts. The environment and the person's experiences in the previous twenty minutes will impact their behavior and communication in your conversation. Every time you are in contact with someone, observe their communication customs and adapt.

- Pay attention to the clues people send you about their customs. Pace and word choice are easy to spot and make your initial adjustments easy.

- Prepare for every conversation with the individual's Tribal Type in mind. Determine the information you should have available, the way you should word your questions, how much small talk to plan for upfront, and the ways in which you should provide value. Then be flexible "in the moment" to ensure you are delivering what they need at that time.

- Appreciate the uniqueness of each person. Some may be more challenging for you to sell and collaborate with than others. Strive to provide value in each of your contacts.

CHAPTER 5

Wait: The Conversation Starts with You

"You usually have to wait for that which is worth waiting for."

—CRAIG BRUCE, **Canadian software developer**

When does the sales conversation really start? If you are focused on Them, your buyers, and following the WIIFT sales system, it starts *before* you engage or connect with your buyer. It begins with your self-discipline to *Wait* before jumping into the conversation.

Wait is the only step of WIIFT that you complete before initiating contact with an existing buyer or a new prospect. *Waiting* keeps you from losing yourself in a robotic process. *Waiting* helps you remain genuine and makes your conversation count.

The *Wait* step's objectives are to maximize the time with your buyer, prepare for the specific conversation, break your preoccupation with everything else, and mentally focus on this buyer and situation.

FIVE ACTIONS TO PREPARE FOR
A CONVERSATION THAT COUNTS

The *Wait* step is the one that is totally in your control. Making time to pause is up to you. Notice I didn't say "taking the time." Often we need to *make* the time and prioritize our preparation.

When you make the time for the Actions of the *Wait* step, you fulfill the main purpose of this step—to begin a productive, value-filled conversation with the buyer. To *Wait* successfully there are five Actions:

1. Eliminate your distractions.

2. Focus on What's in it for *Them* for this conversation.

3. Review notes from previous meetings or research.

4. Check your mirror and materials.

5. Prepare your mind to engage with the buyer.

This *Wait* or final pause before connection may take just moments, or it may take minutes depending upon the meeting you are preparing for. It's not the amount of time you spend, it's how you spend that time.

ACTION 1: ELIMINATE YOUR DISTRACTIONS

What are you doing just before your sales conversations? Many overscheduled sellers are on a phone call, on their computers, or reading their email until the moment they pick up the phone or walk through the buyer's door. They shuffle through papers and check one last time for important calls or messages.

This habit is dangerous. What is most important at that moment is the conversation you are going to have next. That's why *Waiting* starts with you *stopping*. Stopping what? Everything else.

Eliminate distractions so you can be mentally present in your conversations, whether by phone or in person. Turn off your cell phone, turn off your computer screen, physically move away from your desk, or close your door. These precautions will eliminate your distraction, reduce the temptation to multitask, and make it easier to keep your conversation focused where it belongs: on your buyer.

Juggling fast-paced schedules, technology, and multiple expectations leaves many of us stretched for time. We then seek ways to get more done and may adopt the belief that if we work on several things simultaneously—if we multitask—we are more efficient. This is why I often hear sellers brag about how good they are at multitasking and jokingly comment that it works well for them because they have an attention deficit disorder (ADD) personality. (However, I notice that I don't hear top sellers saying this.)

Many people think that we *increase* our productivity by working on several things at the same time. Yet research by Dr. Edward Hallowell, a Massachusetts-based psychiatrist, calls this belief in the efficiencies of multitasking a myth. "It's the great seduction of the information age," he said in an interview on cnet.com in 2008. "You can create the illusion of doing work and of being productive and creative when you're not. You're just treading water." Hallowell's research found that multitasking actually *decreases* productivity and gives us a false sense of what we are really accomplishing.

In his book titled CrazyBusy (Ballantine Books, 2006), Hallowell calls multitasking a "mythical activity in which people believe they can perform two or more tasks simultaneously." In an article published in the *Harvard Business Review* in January 2005, he describes a new condition that mimics ADD, called "attention deficit trait," which he says is "purely a response to the hyperkinetic environment in which we live." (It seems we aren't all ADD after all; it's our response to the activity and rush around us.)

"Never in history has the human brain been asked to track so many data points," writes Hallowell. Yet this challenge "can be controlled only by creatively engineering one's environment and one's emotional and physical health." Limiting your multitasking is essential to achieve the highest levels of productivity and success.

How do we lose so much productivity? Through the time-wasting inefficiencies created by multitasking—and the amount of time lost may surprise you. In 2005, office workers took an average of twenty-five minutes to get back on task after an interruption such as a phone call or answering emails, according to researchers at the University of California at Irvine who monitored these interruptions. Twenty-five minutes of less effective efforts, even after an interruption of just two or three minutes! Think of the number of interruptions we have in a day and do the math; that's a lot of lost time.

If you are thinking, "I would never get anything done if I only focused on one task at a time," you aren't alone. We are multitaskers by nature, and *some* of the multitasking is very effective for us. We can walk and talk at the same time. We *can* talk to a buyer and access our CRM system for information. We can eat and read the newspaper or our newsfeeds—and although I find that I can't remember what I ate, at least I am accomplishing two tasks at the same time.

Multitasking hurts us most when we try to complete two or more tasks that need mental effort at the same time. We cannot break from a mentally challenging task, such as putting together pricing or a recommendation for a buyer, or taking a phone call, and immediately return to the same level of focus and productivity. We lose something in the process—time, an idea, clarity. We then lose the opportunity to give the highest value to everything we are doing.

While this research provides proof to what many of us experience, I do run into the skeptics who challenge the research and argue that it doesn't take twenty-five minutes for them to refocus. When I suggest they personally test the research, and they do so, they acknowledge that it's true. It's why Jason, a client, learned that a straightforward task like inputting customer information into his CRM, begun at 8:15 A.M., wasn't finished until 3:30 P.M. Constant distractions kept him from finishing the top item on his to-do list for nearly the entire workday.

Consider how multitasking affects your selling efforts. When your mind is attempting to focus on other tasks—different buyers, reports you need to complete, a meeting with your manager, or your travel arrangements—it reduces your effectiveness in your conversations and all your actions.

How then do we focus and complete our tasks? Create new habits that eliminate distractions before our sales conversations.

First, identify the common disruptions that keep you from preparing and focusing. Make a note of these disruptions, each time one occurs, for an entire day. Next, determine their importance in the context of your sales efforts—an interruption from your main buyer may be justified, less so those from emails or a coworker. Then develop a plan to eliminate these distractions. Here are some tips for doing so.

Prioritize Each Morning

Address the most important items first, including your preparation for sales calls. A powerful reminder to tackle your most important or challenging tasks first begins with the Mark Twain quote, "Eat a live frog every morning, and nothing worse will happen to you the rest of the day." Best-selling author Brian Tracy used this quote in his book, *Eat That Frog* (Berrett-Koehler Publishers, 2007), suggesting you complete the toughest task first each day to release the energy you would spend on avoiding or thinking about that task the rest of the day. It's easy to think we should tackle the little things first, or knock them out of the way to shorten our list of tasks; however, the big or tough thing occupies our mind and causes us to waste energy and time.

Schedule Time for Preparation

Schedule a specific block of time each day on your calendar for preparation. Oliver, a seller in the consumer products industry, learned quickly how this pays off. He reports that his scheduled block of thirty minutes daily has become invaluable and has led to more efficient conversations—including a typical one-hour weekly meeting successfully concluding in under forty minutes!

Minimize the Inflow

Reduce the number of times your emails are loaded on your computer and on your handheld gadgets. Although most software settings load your messages every three to five minutes, you can change this. When Alice Kemper of Sales Training Consultants changed her settings to receive her emails just once an hour, I thought she was crazy until I saw what it did for her productivity, focus, and quality. Now she is more in control of her time and schedule. While this won't work for everyone, I've found great benefits from thirty minutes of uninterrupted computer time. Unless we have life-or-death matters being emailed to us, why do we need to be interrupted every few minutes with the latest message?

Put Down Your Smartphone

The use of smartphones with their immediate access to email and updates on social media has created a false sense of urgency. Evaluate how often this information helps you with what you need to focus on in the next hour. Then reconsider your need to keep your smartphone on at all times; reduce the frequency of your updates from social media sites and how often you check your cell phone for text messages.

Ask for Time to Finish

When interrupted by someone, ask permission to finish your thought or action or to make a note. Say something like, "Hello, good to hear from you. Can you give me a minute to finish the sentence I was typing so I can then focus on you?" Of course, you should adapt that message to your Tribal Type and situation. Most callers will oblige, and if they don't, then you know it is urgent (if only in their minds).

Multitasking is a bad habit of mine that's difficult to break. When I began to focus on cutting back my multitasking actions, I found it was not just tough for me but also for those around me. They weren't used to me asking for a few minutes to complete something or to schedule time for a discussion. My family struggles with my lack of immediate response as well. They still expect me to react immediately to any interruption, urgent or not.

This new practice of asking for time to finish something lets me complete quality work in shorter periods of time. When I slip into old habits, immediately reacting to everything coming at me, I quickly notice the effect on my conversation success, my ability to fully complete tasks, and my stress level.

Though no one can schedule and control every distraction, we have more control over our multitasking than we think. If you don't respond to someone's email in the next three minutes, will anything earth-shattering happen? Probably not. Resisting that distraction should make you more productive with the time you otherwise would have lost.

Once you have eliminated distractions in the *Wait* step, it's time to turn your focus to *Them*.

ACTION 2: FOCUS ON WHAT'S IN IT
FOR *THEM* IN THIS CONVERSATION

To earn the time and attention of busy buyers, turn your focus to *Them* and their POWNs before your conversation begins. Ensure your conversation—from open to close—is value-filled with preparation that clarifies and defines What's in it for Them.

Putting pen to paper or fingers to a keyboard allows you to map out the objectives, actions, and outcome for your conversation. As televangelist, speaker, motivator, and author Robert H. Schuller said, "Spectacular achievement is always preceded by unspectacular preparation."

To aid you in efficient and productive preparation, use the Quick Prep Tool™. The benefits of using the Quick Prep Tool are best articulated by its users over the past few years. These are actual comments:

- "I have really gained value preparing for each of my calls. This has allowed me to have better conversations and has provided the customer with a better solution."

- "Utilize the Quick Prep Tool for best making a cold call into a warm call."

- "Doing the Quick Prep sheets makes it easier to focus on the conversation on hand and not scramble for the right words. It gives me the opportunity to focus on what the prospect is saying instead of worrying what to say next."

- "Preparation has benefited me greatly. I now make sure to prepare myself ahead of time before I go into a sales call. This helps me to stay focused during the call and enables me to have more control during the sales process."

- "Use of the Quick Prep Tool has enabled more efficient and effective meetings. Meetings are shorter and result in clear decisions being made."

Figure 5–1 presents the first page, WIIFT Quick Prep™ (the second page, Quick Research™, is discussed in the next section of this chapter). Though the Quick Prep Tool looks unspectacular compared to some technology tools, completing it allows you to outline the flow and content of your sales conversation quickly and easily. The first page of the Quick Prep

Figure 5–1 WIIFT Quick Prep™

WIIFT Quick Prep™

Date: _____

Name, Title, Company   Tribal Type©

WAIT   Objective(s) for conversation

Customer POWNs   Need to knows

Value and benefits important to them

INITIATE 3-Step Start notes (greet, why, time/connection questions to open the conversation)

INVESTIGATE Questions to uncover POWNs - problems, opportunities, wants and needs

1

2

3

4

FACILITATE Possible recommendation(s)

Possible objections to discuss

THEN CONSOLIDATE Decision or commitment desired

Follow-up action items
What   Who   When

Tool is designed for you to complete in about five minutes for typical sales calls. This page outlines each of the WIIFT steps with space for you to make notes. It guides you through the conversation before it begins. You can download it at www.conversationsthatsell.com.

As you complete the Quick Prep Tool and identify the objective, the questions you will ask, the information you will share, the objections that may surface, and how you will ask for a decision, keep in mind how the Tribal Types will factor in. Commanders will want lots of details and timelines. Reflectors appreciate seeing the agenda and questions in advance so they can prepare. Achievers want big picture information and will need to be asked more direct questions. And plan plenty of time to talk and connect with Expressers.

ACTION 3: REVIEW NOTES FROM PREVIOUS MEETINGS OR RESEARCH

There's a reason your manager or company leaders request that you document information about your customers—it's invaluable. Use your internal systems and records to stay up-to-date with the buyer's history with you or your company. Then take it further for greater probability of success. Dig deeper into your preparation by using Quick Research, the second page of the Quick Prep Tool, shown in Figure 5–2. The Research page provides thought-starters for identifying additional research points for you to access. Today's technology allows us to easily learn more about buyers, companies, and industries. In addition to reading trade magazines, identify relevant websites to locate information on the buyer and their company. You can locate valuable information on the buying company's website by looking into such details as the company's mission or value statements, industry news or trends, key stakeholders, and recent company business news.

There is a plethora of information now available for business buyers and consumers. Facebook, LinkedIn, and Twitter are great starting places. Begin with a search for the buyer's name and company in search engines to locate the social media sites and forums where they "hang out." Making the time for this research is another layer of preparation.

The Quick Research page guides you through specific considerations to ensure your conversation is relevant to the buyer's current situation. It will help you find further possibilities of new opportunities and new conversation points with the buyer.

Figure 5–2 Quick Research™

Quick Research™   Date: _____

Research outlets (company website, social networking groups, company or industry forums
or community groups, etc.)

Company information

Review the company's website, brochures, annual reports, and marketing documents, as they
provide useful information about:

   Mission or value statement

   Key stakeholders (names, roles, backgrounds)

   Recent company business news (financial results, news releases)

   Specific goals (new markets, expansion, returns to stakeholders, personal goals, etc.)

Industry news and trends

For this buyer, what is in alignment with our solution? What potential value do we offer?

With the additional information you collect, begin identifying how your
solutions align for the buyer. Identify the value you can offer to this person,
company, or situation so you can incorporate that proof into every part of
your conversation.

ACTION 4: CHECK YOUR MIRROR AND MATERIALS

What message about your credibility, professionalism, and your level of interest do you want your buyers to take away when they look at you and the materials you provide? Remember, your appearance, body language, voice, and handouts convey a message. Whether you are face-to-face or on the telephone, it's important to check your mirror and materials before you engage.

Present Yourself Professionally and Credibly

The first indication that you believe your buyers matter to you is made with your personal presentation. For face-to-face meetings, they often see you before you ever speak a word, so take time to ensure you give off the physical impression that you are credible and a professional. Send the message that you find them valuable.

When I was in banking, although our branch managers were very knowledgeable on operations, our products, and customers, their personal presentation did not always match their expertise. To boost their confidence and credibility, we hosted a day-long image event. We brought in speakers who taught dressing for success and gave hair and make-up tips. Then we gave each participant a surprise cash bonus to put the tips into practice. The results were astounding. The managers showed a higher confidence in how they carried themselves and began having more credibility with the business customers. The board of directors declared it a wise investment.

Please don't ignore the tips for face-to-face meetings that follow because you think that "everyone in sales already knows this." You just may find a golden nugget that helps you present your best.

- *Before visiting a company for the first time, ask whoever is scheduling the meeting about the dress code.* You can be sure that the owner of a social media consulting firm learned that lesson when he arrived at a Fortune 500 company presentation (for a $150,000 project) in jeans when everyone in the company wears a tie and jacket. The buying committee even questioned him on his dress. He was quickly moved to the last spot on their list solely based on his disconnect with their culture.

- *Keep your vehicle clean.* If you transport your buyers, they will notice the condition and cleanliness of your vehicle. Your vehicle is an extension of you and who you really are. (Even if you don't transport buyers, note that one company I know of has its receptionist report on the salesperson's vehicle.) Ensure your vehicle is clean inside and out, with no wrappers or papers on the floor or seat. Often participants in my training will help me carry out my supplies at the end of the day. Even though my children are now driving and use my car, their trash or sports clothing would not leave a positive final impression.

- *Ensure your breath and personal hygiene are odor-free.* Although this is common sense, you may be surprised by the stories buyers have shared with me about the odors of sellers. Common complaints are too much cologne, body spray, perfume, coffee breath, and cigarette smoke smells. Take it easy on the sprays and ensure your breath is not offensive.

For telephone conversations, though you may not be seen, checking yourself and the materials you may use, access, or share is important. When conversing by telephone:

- *Eliminate sounds around you whenever possible;* what the caller hears is part of your personal presentation.

- *Organize any documents you may need and have paper and a pen available to take notes or list action items.* The sounds of shuffling papers can make you appear unprepared or disorganized.

- *Clear your throat or have a drink of water to ensure your voice is clear and professional.*

- *Do not eat or chew gum.* Even chewing on a pencil or having a mint in your mouth is heard by the caller.

- *Use a landline when possible to reduce the potential of a bad cell phone connection.*

- *Give your caller your full attention and don't drive and dial.* Tempting as it may be to return calls while on the road, it can also send the message that you are squeezing them in or that you are not focused (and in some states, it's illegal). Pull to the side of the road or into a parking lot before calling a buyer. If you use a Bluetooth or speaker phone, reduce the noises in your vehicle. If someone else is in the vehicle with you, let your caller know. If you aren't behind the wheel, have a pen and paper available for note-taking.

These common-sense tips are effective reminders to ensure you are sharp and ready to make a positive first impression that engages your buyer.

Determine the Right "Stuff" for Your Conversation

Any materials you share with your buyer, virtual or printed, represent the level of professionalism and quality that they will associate with you. So does the "stuff" you bring with you—briefcase, computer, portfolio, marketing materials, and even your pen.

For years I had a laptop that I loved. Unfortunately, the black shiny outside shell was prone to fingerprints. I didn't realize how awful this looked to anyone sitting across from me, including a room full of training-course participants, nor did I think to wipe down my computer top before my presentations. Then one day, when a colleague was presenting and I was in the back of the room observing, I noticed how sloppy the fingerprints looked. It was an easy fix with a computer sleeve, yet it reminded me that *all* my materials and equipment are an extension of my personal presentation and need to look clean and professional.

Evaluate the documents or items you will share with your buyers as you are collaborating to verify whether everything presents the image or message you want. To ensure your "stuff" represents you and your solution positively, first determine what you need for your conversation:

- Brochures
- Technology-based visual aids
- Briefcase
- Handouts

- Samples
- A laptop or tablet
- Demo kit
- Paper, pen, and portfolio

Then evaluate from the buyer's perspective whether each item presents the image you want. If it doesn't present a positive image or advance the relevancy of your solution, make the necessary adjustments to elevate its appearance or eliminate it.

As a buyer I was searching for a marketing advisor/consultant—a huge financial commitment for me at the time. I asked those I trusted for referrals and liked one in particular. We talked by telephone, she put together a recommendation, and we met to review her initial recommendations. Believe me, I was more than a little surprised when she presented her ideas to me on recycled paper from her office.

No, I don't mean store-bought recycled paper; this was paper with unrelated print on the other side. At that point, her credibility as a marketing consultant plunged. I wanted to increase my image and market my company, and that meant help from someone who practiced what they preached. The presentation of her work did not support the top-dollar requirement for her services. Over the years, she had done very good work for other clients in the local area, but she lost my business and willingness to refer her that day.

The right materials may be very different for the different Tribal Types. For Commanders and Reflectors who like to "see and touch," prepare information, supporting data, and a process layout in print. They appreciate tables, graphs, and detail. For Expressers and Achievers, the right material is less detailed, yet it needs to capture their attention. Simplify your message with a picture, simple model, or graphic to keep them focused.

ACTION 5: PREPARE YOUR MIND
TO ENGAGE WITH THE BUYER

The Actions for *Waiting* already shared are tangible and visual. However, your preparation in the *Wait* step includes an extremely important mental Action—preparing your mind.

Consider these situations: Your telephone rings; you arrive at the buyer's location; you are sitting in the lobby of the buyer's business; or you start to dial the telephone—what are you thinking about at that moment? Are you focusing on your buyer or the value you may bring to them? Or are you thinking about some other situation?

Winning conversations—and sales—begin in your head. Study top performers in any discipline and you will find that mental preparation often is cited as critical to their success.

Baseball Hall of Fame player Hank Aaron (who played for my home team, the Milwaukee Brewers) attributed much of his success to his mental preparation—before and during the game. He believed that mental preparation and doing his homework were integral to becoming a great, consistent hitter year after year.

Aaron was an athlete before many of you were born. Yet his message of preparation and homework still holds true today for world-class athletes and sellers. I've heard many top-performing salespeople tell me that they are more successful when they are in the right frame of mind before any sales call.

This pause for mental preparation is the final Action for the *Wait* step because it is the last thing you should do immediately before contact with a buyer. No matter how you connect with your buyers—telephone, email, or a face-to-face visit—your final preparation action should be preparing your mind to engage with them. Waiting and "getting your head in the game" saves both you and your buyer time during your conversations.

Try the following tips for your mental preparation.

Visualize Your Success

While some athletes and artists visualize every part of their upcoming competition or performance, others find that visualizing the outcome is what counts. Use the preparation tips in this chapter to mentally work through the conversation, and then focus on visualizing the benefits of a positive outcome—for you and the buyer.

Develop a Routine

Your routine is a repeatable process, a series of habits you develop to prepare yourself. Determine two actions for your mental prep, then pause and do them before your conversation.

After observing other people's success with mental preparation I created a routine before my training workshops. Instead of making final phone calls, I spend a few minutes thinking and sometimes repeating out loud "it's not about me, it's about them." It keeps my ego intact and focused on the people with whom I am about to engage.

Use Positive Self-talk

Tell yourself that the conversation will be productive and value-filled for all involved.

To illustrate how this self-talk and belief are "heard" by a buyer, I share this real message left on my business line. Of course, identifying information has been altered.

> "Hi Nancy, my name is Jill with ABC Sales. Just so you know this is a sales call, a callback will probably not happen but I'm trying. Uh, we are a blah blah blah company. Our service enables you to blah blah blah, enabling you to blah blah. If this does strike interest you can call me back; the toll free number is 800-111-2222. I am at extension 123. Once again, Jill with ABC Sales, our toll free number is 800-111-2222, extension 123. Oh, and if you'd like to look at our website before calling me, and that's wishful thinking, it's www.abc.abcsales. Thank you, buh-bye."

What do you think Jill's mental prep and self-talk were like before calling me? Dread? Fear? Wishful thinking? It's doubtful her thoughts were positive or focused on success. Now, if her strategy was to make me feel bad for her, it *almost* worked! This is a good example of the confidence discussed in Chapter 1. Jill was not feeling confident and she needed to address that and build her confidence before picking up the phone. She definitely was not able to fake it.

Keep Your Buyer from Ducking Your Efforts

Your attitude toward your buyer is an important aspect of mental preparation. If your goal is to be in collaborative conversations with prospective buyers, consider how your mindset and language about selling impact your buyer's reaction.

Some sales terms create unnecessary barriers between sellers and buyers. For instance, consider the word "pitch." Listen to a group of salespeople and you may hear statements such as:

- "Getting out there to pitch" to someone.

- My "pitch really worked."

- I'm "working on my sales pitch materials."

I also know of sales teams that have a Pitch Book. While I understand the intention of the "pitch" term in sales, its use and connotation often confuse me. In a collaborative selling approach focused on What's in it for Them, how does "pitching someone" fit? Think about it . . . if you are being pitched to, what are your options? You can bat it away, or you can duck.

Neither of these actions are what I want from my buyer. How about you? And what does a buyer think about being "pitched to"? These types of old-school sales terms may contribute to buyers feeling like they are being manipulated. Instead, we can keep our buyers from ducking or batting away our solution by preparing our minds to engage with buyers professionally and collaboratively as we focus on What's in it for Them?

This mental preparation is truly the beginning of the collaborative selling approach. It's the start of you being ready to work with your buyers in a genuine, WiifT-focused, and value-filled approach.

* * *

Your collaborative sales conversation begins with a What's in for *Them* attitude as you review your notes, your Quick Prep Tool, and any other research you have completed. This *Wait* allows you to stop, break your own preoccupation, prepare, and engage your mind so you can focus on Them. Now you are really ready to *Initiate* the conversation with your buyer.

QUICK TIPS FOR PREPARING
FOR YOUR SALES CONVERSATION

- Your conversation success starts with you. Mentally prepare to engage with your buyer before picking up the phone or walking through the door.

- Make the time to prepare on paper. Identify the objective of the conversation, the questions that need to be answered for you and *Them*, the value your solution will provide, and possible objections you will need to work through.

- Adjust the information and materials for the buyer's Tribal Type.

- Research the person, company, and the industry to ensure your conversation will be relevant and value-focused throughout.

- Look in the mirror to ensure your personal presentation is favorable.

- Gather any materials you may need and ensure they represent you and your company positively.

- Eliminate potential distractions before you pick up the phone or enter the meeting place.

CHAPTER 6

Initiate: Win Them at Hello with a Purposeful Start

"It would be interesting to find out what goes on in that moment when someone looks at you and draws all sorts of conclusions."

—Malcolm Gladwell, **author**

After *Waiting,* you are ready to connect with your buyer—the actual start of the two-way conversation. Yet keep in mind that quickly moving into a sales pitch (or any business conversation) can create a "Hold on!" response from the buyer that ends the conversation before it really gets started. Instead, engage the buyer in a conversation focused on Them—with a purposeful start.

The *Initiate* step of WIIFT opens the door to a value-filled conversation that connects you with buyers to build trust, break their preoccupation with other matters, and earn the right for you to ask questions. Purposely *Initiating* your conversation ensures that *this* conversation will count for both of you. These are the first moments that determine much of the value for the rest of that conversation.

FIVE ACTIONS TO ENSURE A PURPOSEFUL CONVERSATION START

Though you are prepared for the conversation, the buyer may not be. I don't know of any buyer who sits around with pen in hand waiting for you, even for a scheduled appointment. Do you?

For most situations, you can expect that the buyer is doing something else until the moment you call or enter their office. *Initiating* is important for both of you; your preparation keeps you from wasting time—yours and theirs. The five Actions that open the conversation, and the opportunity, with purpose in the *Initiate* step are:

1. Greet.

2. Explain why you are connecting.

3. Ask questions to engage and get them talking.

4. Use appropriate eye contact and open ears.

5. Focus on what they are communicating—words and intent.

Though there is considerable flexibility in how you *Initiate* the conversation, there is a method to the madness of starting the conversation. I call it the Three-Step Start.

The Three-Step Start

The start of your conversation is not just about you. It's about you *and* Them! It's your first approach toward a collaborative and valuable conversation and sales process.

The first three Actions of the *Initiate* step—the Three-Step Start—are your guide to what you say or write to start the conversation. These Actions, which can be adapted to *Initiate* any conversation, connect you to Them quickly.

For most situations, you can expect that the buyer has yet to engage in the purpose of your conversation, let alone the specific topic. When they first hear from you or see you, most buyers have these unstated questions in mind:

- Who are you? Are you credible?

- Why are you contacting me?

- Is this worth my time?

- Who is this really about? Do you want to pitch something at me?

Your ability to answer these questions quickly breaks their preoccupation with these questions and engages Them in your conversation. The buyer's unspoken questions need to be addressed efficiently and purposely *every* time because connecting Them to *each* conversation earns you the green light to proceed.

The Three-Step Start answers the buyer's unstated questions, for example:

- "Good afternoon Carol, I am Richard Dover with Market Planners. We scheduled time to discuss your upcoming annual meeting and how we can take the burden of the planning off your to-do list. Does this time still work for you? *(Pause for response.)* No? Can we reschedule for tomorrow morning at 9 A.M.?"

- "Good morning Mrs. Jones, I am with ABC Company and we supplement the product life cycle process to increase the variability of cost in your overhead. I'm calling today to ask you a few questions to see if it makes sense for our companies to do business together. How does that sound to you?" *(Pause for response.)*

- "Hello and thank you for inviting me to talk with your group today. I am Mike Haubrich of Financial Service Group. We partner with our clients through life's transitions to keep their financial peace of mind. During our sixty minutes together today we will share with you three important items that you need to know to ensure your investments are safe for your financial well-being. Let's start with introductions. Would you please share your name and tell us what's the best financial decision you've ever made?"

- "Good afternoon, Mr. Reimer. This is Kayla Green with Enviro-Works. I read in the local paper that you recently broke ground for a new office complex. Congratulations. We specialize in commercial landscape services that allow you to reduce in-house maintenance costs and comply with the city's new environmental regulations. I'd like to ask a few questions to determine whether one of our programs might meet your needs. Do you have fifteen minutes to explore your situation? *(Pause for response.)* Thanks, I'll ask only two questions and then you can decide if we should schedule more time."

You can adjust the Three-Step Start for consumers, businesses, C-level executives, cold or warm calls, and the number of people in the conversation. Although the primary focus in this chapter is on the face-to-face conversation, you can also use the Three-Step Start on the telephone, in written communication, and with groups—each of which will be covered later in this chapter.

You should adapt and adjust the Three-Step Start for your own personal, value-filled conversation starter depending upon:

- Your relationship with the buyer.

- The objective of the conversation.

- The buyer's Tribal Type.

- The mode of contact: face-to-face, telephone, or written.

- The number of people involved.

- Whether you are initiating the conversation or on the receiving end of an inbound contact.

While the first three Actions that make up the Three-Step Start are central to the *Initiate* step, the final two Actions guarantee you communicate effectively from the beginning of your conversation until the end.

ACTION 1: GREET

The first words spoken set the tone for the rest of the conversation. In the Three-Step Start, Greet is the first Action and it sets a positive, collaborative tone for your conversation. It's a short Action that addresses one of the unstated questions buyers have upon contact: "Who are you?"

Tell Them Who You Are

Clearly introduce yourself with these specifics:

- *A salutation.* Begin your conversations with a positive, sincere greeting; for example, "Hello." "Good morning/afternoon." "Great to see you." "Hola!" Address them by name when possible. For first contacts, be more formal by using their proper names; don't shorten someone's name unless they have given you permission.

- *Your name.* Adapt this for your buyer's familiarity with you, your personal style, and comfort level. Some sellers just use their first name while others always use both their first and last names. Your company may have a preference. State your name clearly and add an interesting connection if possible. For instance, if your name was Joann Sleight you could say your name and then make it memorable by saying "Sleight, like Santa's sleigh with a T added." If you have an unusual or hard-to-pronounce first or last name, you may find that is a great conversation opener.

- *Company name.* Identify your company by name and by your solution, if needed. Buyers don't want to rack their brain trying to make the connection. You could say, Nancy Bleeke with Sales Pro Insider and Genuine Sales. Or Matt Michaels with Rexnord, maker of the Thomas Coupling.

Adjust your greeting to your Type, the situation, and the buyer. Don't assume they know or remember you or your company.

Make the First Moments Count

Purposeful first moments in every conversation are invaluable. They demonstrate you are prepared, organized, focused on Them, and most importantly, that you won't waste their time. A sincere greeting immediately connects them to you as a person and begins that important dynamic called *buyer engagement.*

How much time do you have to engage your buyer? While it varies, their first impression of you affects the level and speed of the engagement. And this impression is formed quickly. When you are face to face, first impressions are formed by your overall approach, including how you look, whether your face is smiling or stern, and the items you have with you.

Research by Janine Willis and Alexander Todorov of Princeton University in 2005 found that first impressions are made in between 100 and 500 *milli*seconds. They discovered that it only takes a tenth of a second to form an impression of a stranger from their face and that longer exposures don't significantly alter those impressions, although the longer exposure might boost confidence in their initial judgments.

Five hundred milliseconds is just a brief moment. To make that moment positive, be prepared to engage in a meaningful start to the conversation, as discussed in Chapter 5.

ACTION 2: EXPLAIN WHY YOU ARE CONNECTING

To quickly address the buyer's unstated questions, "What's this about?" and "Is this worth my time?", briefly explain the reason for the call or meeting. This is the time to share the agenda or to confirm the agenda if it was set beforehand.

For existing relationships, tell Them why you are connecting and What's in it for Them (the WiifT): "I'm calling to find out if you were able to review the information I shared regarding how you can decrease the number of dropped calls you were experiencing."

This opener is different than a valueless starter such as, "I'm just checking in to see if you have read what I sent you about the new cell phone." Including the WiifT focuses the buyer on why they should make the time to talk with you.

Fill Your Introduction with Value

New contacts need more than just an introduction. They need proof—the umbrella over WIIFT—to justify and validate why they should talk with you. This *value statement* is a proof point for who you are, what this is about, and What's in it for Them.

The value statement I'm talking about is a succinct sentence or two that states the value they can expect from your time together or what you and your solution will provide.

Value statements provide context and a WiifT to answer their unstated question, "Is this worth my time?" For example:

- "We just finished a project for a client where we were able to fill their pipeline with 250 percent more leads and shorten their sales cycle from six to four months."

- "It's a pleasure to meet you, I appreciate the opportunity to assist you with your employee development and growth opportunity goals."

- "Our customers save between 5 and 15 percent with our home insurance compared to other insurance company policies."

- "This is our callback to discuss your retirement planning, and how our work with individuals provides them with financial stability today and the retirement lifestyle they want tomorrow fits with your plan."

- "Today we're discussing sales training and how you would benefit from additional sales, like our Canadian customer who sold a sustainable $2.5 million in services in the first six weeks of implementing our sales system."

- "We scheduled this time to discuss your widget performance and how our widget provides cost savings of up to 18 percent over what most facilities are currently spending."

A simple way to create your value statement is to combine three components into a relevant statement:

Value statement = Action + Solution + Result

Building a value statement is not as difficult as you might think. Use words like *build, increase/decrease, save, address (the problem of),* or *provide* to describe the action. Add words like *financial stability, market share, sustainable growth, low-cost alternatives,* and *comfort and peace of mind,* to describe the solution. Then describe results in the form of numbers (*dollars, ROI, savings*), impact on a relationship (*sharing, togetherness, working through problems*), or emotional benefits (*less stress, more happiness, better health*), and include *specific testimonials* and *names of important users* when possible.

Perhaps the hardest part of developing a powerful value statement is finding appropriate measurement of results. If you don't have readily available metrics, gather them by talking to existing customers and asking them:

• Why do you use this solution?

• What made you decide to first purchase it?

• What results have you realized from using it?

You can also ask other successful sales reps what value they attach to your solution and about their experiences with buyers' success and results. Or interview someone in your marketing department on applicability and documented results achieved.

And, of course you can also tap into your own experiences and knowledge by answering the following questions:

• What problems do I solve for buyers?

• What opportunities have I helped my buyers capture?

• What are the results my solution has achieved for my buyers?

• What needs are addressed with my solution?

• What happens when customers don't implement or purchase my solution?

When stating why you are contacting the buyer, connect the reason to a WiifT or include an appropriate value statement.

ACTION 3: ASK QUESTIONS TO
ENGAGE AND GET THEM TALKING

An easy way to turn the focus to Them and get them talking as early as possible is by asking questions. There are two kinds of questions to use in the *Initiate* step, Time and Connection.

Time to Talk?

Show that you value their time by addressing it very early in the conversation. By addressing time, you can determine the pace of the conversation, reschedule if necessary, and alleviate any fears or concerns they have about time:

- "We have thirty minutes scheduled. Does that sound okay?"

- "So that we make good use of our time, how much time did you plan for our conversation?"

- "Does this time still work for you?"

Their response to the time question tells you if you can move forward or if you need to reschedule to a more convenient time. It's a courtesy many sellers skip because well-meaning marketers and sales managers—fearful of a *no*—tell them to never ask for time. While you can eliminate a *no* now, if you push a conversation on Them that they haven't agreed upon, how far will you get? I believe asking for time shows respect for them and demonstrates your desire to collaborate and make it about *Them*.

Tribal "Time" Customs

Address the issue of time—in a way that is appropriate to each Tribal Type—to demonstrate that you are considerate, paying attention to time, and not going to waste *their* time.

Achievers always have time on their mind. Confirming or asking about it reassures Them that you will keep things moving and communicates how much of their time you will take. Often they will say, "We have sixty minutes scheduled but I hope we can finish in forty so I can get to my next meeting." You'll know it's a valuable conversation when they stop looking at their clock.

Commanders want to control the time and tell you how much time is needed or available. They will also expect that you stick to whatever time you planned. Pay close attention to time and do time check-ins throughout the conversation.

Reflectors need to know they will have time to really have a conversation, get information, and have their questions answered. Their concern is whether you are going to rush them. By confirming and clarifying time you reduce this concern.

Expressers may not think of time. They are flexible and generous with the time they will give you. Your job is to keep the conversation on track to accomplish your objective.

Once you know the time situation for the buyer, whether it is five minutes or an hour and a half, you are then able to adjust the pace and possibly your agenda.

Turn the Focus to *Them* with Connection Questions

When you have permission for time with the buyer, or time confirmation, ask a *connection question*. These are relevant questions to engage the person and *connect* with Them. Connection questions are about Them, not your solution, and could be about anything from a common point in your backgrounds to their experiences in their job or company. This is a momentary stop to engage the buyer as a person, before the investigation into their POWNs.

Asking connection questions—and hearing their response—is your opportunity to break their preoccupation, to get a feel for their Tribal Type and their level of openness to you, and to find out more about Them. If they give a short, curt response to the connection question, it's time to move forward to the *Investigate* step.

While sometimes it is necessary to begin the agenda items after confirming time, there are many willing buyers who *want* to connect with you first. You may be surprised at how many buyers will engage with you when given the opportunity to do so. The buyer's experience and value is enhanced when you give Them the opportunity to engage with you personally.

The connection question could be an occasion you shared, opinions on their company, the market, your industry, the time of year, the location, something that just happened in the news, who they are associated with, past experiences, other interests, their role, the status of something you both know about, or a connection of topics from past conversations such as work projects, family, hobbies, vacation, or a work transition.

However you prefer to start a sales conversation doesn't matter as much as how *They* like to begin and what *They* want to talk about. That's how knowing a buyer's Tribal Type can guide you to the right question to ask. Depending on the Type, asking about the weather, family, or weekend plans might work—or should be avoided! Plan your connection questions to be relevant to Them by reviewing notes from previous conversations or topics you find from the company website or social networking sites. You can also ask others who know the person or situation to identify the most probable and relevant questions for *this* conversation and person.

The buyer's environment provides clues for connection questions, whether it's a home, office, or vehicle. You may find pictures, memorabilia, or plaques that give you a conversation opener.

Take the seller who noticed a picture of the buyer in a fishing boat. Their conversation about fishing consumed 75 percent of their time together and produced a time for the next appointment before the meeting ended. That second meeting was easy, the seller told me, and a sale was made.

Achievers and Commanders often respond to connection questions that are more business-related and less focused on personal things. For instance:

- "How did last quarter finish for your team or company?"

- "In doing research, I noticed that you've been in the industry a long time. What kinds of changes have you seen?"

- "Last time we spoke, you mentioned that the company was starting a new product development project. How's that going?"

- "How is _____ working out?"

These are business-related questions that stop short of focusing on agenda specifics.

For consumer sales situations, ask Achievers and Commanders connection questions such as:

- "What did you think of _____ (*insert* an event, relevant news, our last meeting)?"

- "How long have you been interested in (*or* searched for) _____ (*insert* the product)?"

For Reflectors and Expressers, ask connection questions about themselves, others they know, or how they feel about something in the news, the weather, their family, or their company. For example:

- "Jim Smith, who referred me to you, said he used to work with you. How long did you work together?"

- "How was your weekend?"

- "I see that your phone number is an Arizona number. How long have you lived there?"

- "You mentioned in your LinkedIn profile that you graduated from the University of Toronto. What led you to attend that college?"

For consumer sales situations, ask Reflectors and Expressers questions such as:

- "How do you feel about _____ (*insert* an event, relevant news, your last meeting)?"

- "What do you like or dislike about _____ (*insert* their job, location)?"

- "Tell me about your family."

TIMELY TIP

Discussing religion or politics is dangerous and frequently a conversation-stopper. Criticizing or complaining about others, including your competition, can also shut down a conversation quickly—you never know the buyer's connection to your competition! Possibly the biggest conversation stopper is you doing most or all of the talking. Give *Them* the opportunity to talk as soon as possible.

A caution about connection questions: You may get a very short or abrupt answer. If you do, then it's time to seek permission to move into the agenda or topic they agreed to talk with you about or ask them additional questions, if necessary, about the objective of your visit. That's when you are officially in the *Investigate* step of WIIFT.

Connection questions *Initiate* the conversation and the buyer's responses provide insight and a connection for you to build from.

∗ ∗ ∗

The *Initiate* step is your first opportunity to engage the buyer and begin learning about Them and what is important to Them. When you *Initiate* your conversations, adapt the Three-Step Start to the situation. You may find that sometimes using all three steps in quick succession for outbound, unplanned cold contacts works well. For most conversations, though, this is a joint effort; you greet, listen to their response and return their greeting, explain why or remind them why you are connecting, let them contribute their thoughts to the objective and agenda, and then ask a question to engage Them.

Successful Initiations are more than *what* you say in the Three-Step Start. *How* you communicate at the beginning of your conversation is just as important. Listening, eye contact, and focusing on Them are needed for you to engage and connect with the buyer.

ACTION 4: USE APPROPRIATE EYE CONTACT AND OPEN EARS

Eye contact and open ears are important pieces to the success of your start. We are more connected in our communication with the buyer when we incorporate our eyes and ears from the first moment of contact.

Use Visual Cues to Engage

Make eye contact is an age-old communication tip that always is current. Your eyes are a powerful tool to make a deeper connection and ensure you are clearly communicating your message.

Eye contact is essential for connecting in face-to-face conversations, and "How much eye contact should I make?" is a real (and very tough) question! There isn't a formula for eye contact that we can easily put into practice. Using *appropriate* eye contact is the key.

Appropriate eye contact is achieved when you pay attention to the buyer's signals to determine what is comfortable for them. Some people are *not* comfortable with direct eye contact, while others will stop talking if you look away. I've had conversations where I had a hard time looking down to take notes because of the buyer's intense eye contact.

Cultural and gender differences also are a factor. I've noticed that women professionals can acceptably make more eye contact with both genders than men can. You'll need to find the right amount of eye contact for each situation by paying attention.

What you do with your eyes sends a message about what is important to you. Your eyes are beams that illuminate what you are focused on. When you focus on Them, you demonstrate that you are paying attention and that They matter.

Appropriate eye contact allows you to see their reaction as you *Initiate* your conversation and quickly make adjustments to make it most comfortable for that buyer. Matching eye contact with open ears makes this easier.

Listen with Open Ears

Many sellers talk too much, which creates a conversation dynamic that is more *tell* than collaboratively *sell* focused. Though we do need to be ourselves and position who we are and why they should talk with us, we can also quickly talk ourselves out of a sales opportunity.

Buyers don't have time to waste. They will shut you out or close the conversation if they think you are wasting their time by talking at Them.

Use open ears to make ear contact and keep the conversation open. Some call this listening. I use the expression "ear contact" because the term is more descriptive of effective, active listening. Our ears can be used very effectively to connect to their words, intent, and emotion, and therefore their hot buttons that may make or break our sale.

Open ears also means that when you ask a question, you need to do more than just wait to talk. You need to pause and listen for the response. The pausing is important. If you're like most people, after asking a question, you may only wait between one and three seconds before you ask another question, repeat the question, or move along.

I know I've been guilty of this! That's why I appreciate that many years ago a Reflector shared with me that when someone—me at the time—asks a question and then tries to rush her through an answer, it's extremely frustrating and shuts down her thought process. This closes any opportunity for her to meaningfully contribute to the conversation, ideas, and solutions. She reminded me that I need to pause, especially if I've asked a thought-provoking or detailed question, and wait for the response.

In my observations, I find that some people need between ten and twenty seconds to formulate *and* begin to verbalize their response. That's a l-o-n-g time to remain quiet and stay focused without multitasking, answering the question yourself, or beginning to ask other questions. However, the response is usually well worth the discomfort of being silent for a short time.

For telephone conversations a long pause becomes uncomfortable and the buyer begins to wonder if you hung up on them. A pause of six to eight seconds is effective for telephone conversations.

If you need further proof of the importance of listening, the Gearner Group's research based on interviews with over 850 sales professionals found an 88 percent correlation with sales success and active listening. Effective active listening skills were observed in 93 percent of those in the top group of sales, compared to 8 percent in the lowest percentiles.

Ear contact is most important in situations where you don't have a visual connection. To make good ear contact use open ears in the *Initiate* step and in the whole conversation:

- *Listen without distractions.* Stop multitasking!

- *Take notes on key points to help you focus in this conversation.* Then refer to these notes in your preparation for future conversations.

- *Postpone evaluating what they are saying and just listen.* Don't start mentally composing your answer while they're still talking.

- *Paraphrase the information they share.* You will listen more carefully when you know you need to paraphrase the information.

Using open ears allows you to "hear" opportunities that you can then translate into sales.

ACTION 5: FOCUS ON WHAT THEY ARE COMMUNICATING—WORDS AND INTENT

The last Action for the *Initiate* step is to focus on what They are communicating—words and intent. This continues key aspects of the *Wait* step message—eliminate distractions and multitasking in order to be present in *this* conversation with *this* person at *this* time.

Focusing on words and intent expands the ideas of Action 4 (appropriate eye contact and open ears) to also pay attention to the *unspoken* communication. To hear what they are intending with their responses, listen for the emotions, motives, and energy associated with what they talk about. These are all signals about what is important to Them.

Look for Unspoken Messages

Your eyes are important throughout the conversation for more than just looking at the eyes of the buyer. Observe everything about their movements and environment.

You will get key information about their real message when you pay attention "in the moment." Notice their pace and body language; be aware of hesitations, nervousness, and confidence. These valuable unspoken messages let you gauge the probability of the sales opportunity, allowing you to spend your time on the most probable opportunities in your pipeline.

The president of a company I spoke with several times scheduled a meeting with me and his management team to consider a custom leadership and sales training solution. The managers were open to the solution and we were discussing next steps when a woman came in and announced that the owner wanted to know the purpose of this meeting and why he wasn't invited.

The president excused herself and left the room. The managers never said a word, but their body language—eyes darting about, some nervous throat clearing, and looking at each other and their papers instead of me—demonstrated their desire to end the conversation quickly. The president returned a few minutes later to announce that they "had some internal work to do before they could continue the conversation with me." Though the president exchanged a few emails in the following weeks, we never met again. The managers' unspoken messages at my meeting confirmed that this opportunity was dead and kept me from spending a lot of time pursuing it further.

Earn the Right to Move Forward in the Conversation

All the Actions of *Initiate* lead you to the ultimate objective, which is to *earn the right to move forward* in the conversation. When you focus on engaging and connecting with Them (as opposed to going into a product pitch), the buyer is more open to the conversation shifting to a discussion on their POWNs. They will give you permission to move into the *Investigate* step and provide the information that qualifies them and the potential opportunity.

So, how do you earn the right to move forward? By connecting with the buyer. By showing that you are listening to Them. By respecting their time limits and the customs of their particular Tribe. And your preparation makes all of those things easier.

After listening to their responses to connection questions, it is easy to segue into the Investigation with a comment such as, "It is good to hear that you enjoy your job. Are you ready to move to the specific questions I have for you today?" or "I understand you are pressed for time, let's get to the reason we're talking."

The subtle feel of the way you approach the conversation differentiates you from the competition, and sets you up to collaboratively *Investigate* the buyers' POWNs productively. When they have let you in and engaged in the conversation with you, it's a good start to collaboration.

ADJUST YOUR INITIATION TO THE SITUATION

So far, I've focused on face-to-face conversations. With a few adjustments you can use the Three-Step Start to *Initiate* telephone, written, and group sales conversations.

Telephone Three-Step Starts

With minor adjustments, the Three-Step Start is effective when *Initiating* telephone sales conversations. The primary difference is that your voice is the key tool in quickly engaging and connecting instead of your first visual impression.

First impressions on the telephone are created from the first words you say, the tone of your voice, and background noises. One easy way to make a favorable impression in telephone conversations is to smile.

Have you ever heard that people can hear you smile? It's true! A 2008 study through the University of Portsmouth in England found that smiles could be discerned without visual cues. They found that not only could callers identify if the telephone speaker was smiling, they were able to determine the *type* of smile.

I didn't realize there were different types of smiles but the study participants were able to discern a Duchenne smile, which is a full smile involving the crinkling of the eyes, from a non-Duchenne smile, where the eyes are not involved. A Duchenne smile is considered a more natural and genuine smile. This research is proof that the smile in your voice is heard by the person on the other end.

Additional ways to make a positive first impression over the telephone include:

- *Keep the tone and pitch of your voice steady, upbeat, and energetic.*

- *Minimize or eliminate interruptions.*

- *Verbalize what you are doing throughout the conversation.* If you enter information using the keyboard, tell the buyer what you are doing so they don't wonder about it; for example: "You will hear me clicking on the keyboard as I look up that information for you." Or, "I'm making a note on what you are telling me."

- *Minimize unnecessary noises.* Shuffling papers, clicking a pen, or typing on a keyboard are all sounds heard by the caller. As I conduct phone interviews for sales reps, I hear candidates turn on/off water, eat, open and close doors, and more.

Outbound Three-Step Starts for buyers with whom you have had previous contact are the same as with face-to-face conversations you *Initiate.*

Your preparation for cold calls is a little different in that you need to adjust the Three-Step Start so that it's as specific and relevant to the buyer and situation as possible with the information that you have. Most important is the value statement that will resonate with Them. The Ask questions need to be more direct to the topic so you do not waste their time:

"Hi John. This is Nancy Bleeke of Sales Pro Insider. The reason I'm calling is because I noticed you were hiring salespeople. One of your competitors hires their sales talent through our services and I thought this might be of interest to you. Do you have ten minutes to discuss your hiring and whether we might help you? *(Pause.)* Wonderful. Please tell me the types of positions you are responsible for hiring."

Inbound telephone conversations give you an advantage because the person calling has proactively contacted you, presumably *wanting* to talk with you. The objective of *Initiating* the conversation from your end remains the same: connect with the buyer to build trust, engage them to break their preoccupation with other matters, and earn the right to ask questions to clarify and discover how you or your solution can address the POWN they called about.

Though the buyer is calling you, your purposeful initiation allows you to take control and be more than a reactive order-taker. You can quickly set the stage to be *in* the conversation with Them and earn the right to expand the conversation to discover POWNs that increase your sales probability and opportunity.

Here is how the Three-Step Start works for inbound calls with some practical suggestions to start your part of the conversation positively:

1. *Greet* with a welcoming salutation identifying your company and your name.

2. *Explain* that you appreciate their call.

3. *Ask* for their name when possible and how you can assist them.

Use the three steps in the order and flow that fits your situation:

- "Good morning and thank you for calling The Green Lawn Service. This is Karla. How may I assist you?"

- "Hello, I appreciate your call to the Center. This is Kevin. What can I help you with today?"

- "Greetings. This is Jackson with the Local Cell Company. Thank you for calling. May I have your name?"

Add value to inbound sales opportunities by focusing on the person on the other end of the call. Create a genuine connection with the buyer, assessing how they want to communicate with you at that moment, and moving forward to earn the right to open the sales opportunity.

Written Conversation Starts

Written correspondence allows you time to make the Three-Step Start just right. This pays off because you have a very short time to grab their attention before they press the delete key, toss the letter in the trash, or add the message to their long to-do list to address later!

Your written Three-Step Start should include:

- *Greet* with a salutation that includes their name so it doesn't look like a form message.

- *Explain* specifically why you are writing. This should include your introduction and any connection you have to them if they don't know you.

- *Ask* for their attention or the request for action sooner rather than later.

Make a positive start, whether it is an email or a paper letter, by:

- Using a relevant subject line.

- Presenting a clear, concise, and logical message.

- Clearly requesting or stating the action you desire—the reason for the connection.

- Giving Them the option to respond to you by email, postal letter, or telephone. Include all your contact information. (You might be surprised who will pick up the phone and call you!)

- Ending with a personalized salutation and your name.

Initiating to a Group

If you sell to groups of two or more people—including couples—adjust the Three-Step Start to engage the entire group.

Group sales present additional dynamics that impact your conversations. For example, some people will act differently in the group setting than they did in a one-on-one conversation. At the beginning of a group sales conversation, to my great surprise, an Achiever with whom I previously conversed in quick, time-constrained meetings was talkative, friendly, and wanted to ensure that everyone from his team was part of the conversation.

To make the group *Initiation* successful, don't assume that each person knows:

- Who you are.

- Why you are meeting with them (the topic).

- Why they are there.

- The objective of the conversation.

Use the Three-Step Start to focus the entire group, engage them, and move the conversation forward:

1. *Greet* by using a salutation, your name, and company name.

2. *Explain* why the group is talking or meeting.

    - Use a summary statement or PPT slide to focus on why you are meeting.

    - Acknowledge who you have met/talked with prior to the meeting.

    - Prepare a value statement that connects with different Tribal Types. If telling a story or testimonial, use names and metrics and be sure to include supporting proof.

    - Clarify the time scheduled for the meeting with an agenda or overview of what will be covered.

3. *Ask* questions to engage each person. If the group is small, ask each person to answer a question such as "What do you want to ensure we cover today?" or "What can we do to make this a good use of your time?"

    If you do not have time or there are too many people, engage individuals within the group by:

    - Asking them to take notes.

- Mentally involving them with a story, an image on the PPT or brochure, or with reflective questions.

* * *

Your purposeful and prepared Initiation allows you to capture the attention of the group and focus all of them on the same page and topic.

QUICK TIPS FOR INITIATING YOUR CONVERSATION

- Consistently use the Three-Step Start—Greet, Explain, and Ask—to begin your conversations. Adjust the way you use the Start for the specific situation and Tribal Type.

- Prepare and practice how you will begin a conversation, especially for new buyer situations.

- In group situations, ask a connection question that gives each person the opportunity to engage if they so choose.

- Clearly state your objective and tie the reason why into a WiifT.

- When buyers say they have time but hurry up, or that they have just a minute, use the little time you have with them to reschedule a better time.

- Pause after you ask a question. Rushing will not make them want to talk more. Focus on waiting ten to fifteen seconds when face to face and six to eight seconds on the phone. Smile whether face to face or on the telephone. Let them see and hear that you are welcoming and glad to be talking with Them.

- Be on time, confident, and positive.

- Look for the unspoken messages and the intent, emotions, and motivations by paying attention to their body language and the environment.

CHAPTER 7

Investigate: Investigation or Interrogation?

"Talk to people about themselves and they will listen for hours."
—BENJAMIN DISRAELI

Transitioning from one step to the next in WIIFT is easy. After connecting with the buyer and earning the right to talk business in the *Initiate* step, it's a seamless move into the *Investigate* step. And this is where your real focus becomes transparent. Will your focus on Them be collaborative or will it turn the conversation into an interrogation?

The *Investigate* step identifies and explores the buyer's POWNs—problems, opportunities, wants, and needs; it qualifies the buyer and clarifies their sense of urgency in addressing their POWNs. Keeping the focus on your buyer is easy when you ask the right questions. The questions you ask are a gauge of what you know. When you use your knowledge to guide Them in clarifying their POWNs and discovering new ones, you provide extra value for Them.

Asking the right questions to open collaboration possibilities is a skill that requires expertise, patience, and preparation. These questions ensure your investigation does not become an interrogation—and there's a big difference between these two approaches. An *investigation* involves researching information in advance, looking for clues, and examining a situation. An *interrogation* involves asking direct, pointed questions focused on a specific course of action determined by the interrogator. When I hear the word interrogation, I picture a bright light shining on a heavily sweating interviewee struggling to answer very direct and leading questions. No one wants to be that sweaty interviewee on the receiving end of an interrogation—especially today's buyers who already have enough pressures.

Your ability to be an effective and collaborative investigator greatly advances your sales opportunities. Helping the buyer clarify their POWNs is valuable and increases the likelihood of them wanting to work with you again and again.

Five Actions to Investigate Compelling POWNs™

Don't be fooled into thinking that all you need to do is get the buyer to talk. That's not enough; you need to actively listen, clarify, add context to your questions, and adapt the questions as needed to keep the conversation collaborative.

Successful completion of the *Investigate* step is more probable when you first prepare by identifying the information that you and They need to uncover, write the questions that will uncover the information, and then use the following five Actions during your conversation:

1. Ask relevant open-ended questions.

2. Listen actively.

3. Ask follow-up questions.

4. Paraphrase what They have stated.

5. Qualify and confirm that They want to discuss a solution before moving on.

Each Action is important for a collaborative, value-filled investigation.

ACTION 1: ASK RELEVANT, OPEN-ENDED QUESTIONS

The investigation with the buyer is an opportunity to prove to Them your expertise, professionalism, and character. You prove these qualities when you ask relevant, open-ended questions.

Begin this Action by first identifying the information you need to know and your buyer needs to discover. For example, you need to determine if they are a qualified buyer and they may need to discover that they have a risk for something that they were not aware of. With a clear understanding of the information that needs to be discovered and uncovered, you can more easily develop potential questions to ask.

Open-ended questions solicit more information than closed questions. Open-ended questions draw out facts, emotions, motivations, and the degree of urgency. The right questions solicit great information, get the person talking, show your expertise, and allow you both to identify potential opportunities.

Closed questions ask the buyer for one piece of information or data. They narrow the focus of the conversation. "Do you have a problem with your _____?" is a direct, closed question that may lead to qualifying the buyer, but it doesn't lead to an open collaborative conversation.

Open-ended questions begin with words like "who," "what," "how," and "why"—for example, in questions such as:

- "What would happen if _____?"

- "What approach would you use to _____?"

- "How would you use _____?"

- "What is the relationship between _____?"

- "What evidence have you found that _____?"

- "Why is _____?"

- "What could be changed or improved in _____?"

- "Where do you see _____?"

- "What way would you design _____?"

- "What outcome would you predict for _____?"

- "How could you select _____?"

- "How do you prioritize _____?"

- "What information would you use to support _____?"

You can also open the conversation with a request for information such as:

- "Please tell me about _____."

- "Help me understand _____."

- "Please share with me _____."

These *Investigation* thought-starters help buyers discover and discuss important information you will need to first identify if there is an opportunity, and then connect your solution to their POWNs.

✓ TIMELY TIP

A caution about asking "why" questions: Although "why" is a powerful way to find reasons and get explanations, it can also seem interrogative, aggressive, and manipulative. Use "why" only after trust is established and your conversation is collaborative.

Uncover Problems, Opportunities, Wants, and Needs

The POWNs are what we need to uncover and sometimes, more importantly, help Them discover. The buyer's problems, opportunities, wants, and needs are all potential sales possibilities.

Uncover the problems that are hurting or hindering the buyer in some way. This is the "pain" that may create enough discomfort that they are open to a solution to alleviate it. Sometimes buyers aren't comfortable discussing their problems because they believe that leaves them vulnerable to being "sold to." If you focus only on their pain, you risk alienating them or making them so uncomfortable that they won't want to speak with you again. In addition, discussing problems is not always viable. Perhaps the buyer doesn't recognize a problem or want to address existing ones. Some people also like to phrase their problems more gently, calling them issues or challenges—well, the term doesn't matter as long as they talk about the information, so use the terms "issues" and "challenges" if necessary. And in this case, focusing on opportunities might work especially well.

Uncover the opportunities your buyers are dreaming of, don't know about, or have no idea how to capitalize on. Get them talking about what they wish for, how they would like things to be, their vision for possibilities, and their ideas. Use your expertise in your industry to discuss opportunities they may not be aware of.

Uncover your buyers' wants. What your buyers want may be more powerful than what they need. Wants tap into emotions and often influence their sense of urgency in taking action.

Uncover your buyers' needs. What do they need to do, have, stop, or start? What must happen or be acquired? Not everybody has a specific need—or they don't perceive that they do—which may mean that they feel they would be wasting their time reviewing your solution. Before moving on to other sales possibilities, explore potential problems, opportunities, or wants.

Often I'm asked, "What's the difference between a want and a need?" The simple answer, as an engineering seller said: "I may need a vehicle, but I want a Ferrari." A need is a necessity, a want is most often a desire or emotionally driven need.

You open sales opportunities when you discuss more than problems or needs with your buyers. For instance, a group in the financial services industry shared information with me about their current sales training program. They mentioned how comfortable they were facilitating the sessions, how the developer had customized the course for them five years earlier, and how satisfied they were with their current process. All their responses suggested they had no problem or need for my solution.

Then I asked how they kept the skills sharpened after the original seminar and they explained they spent considerable time creating reinforcing activities, messages, and support materials. That was my opportunity opener! I used their unacknowledged needs to explore the value they would find in having such items developed for them. We were able to collaborate on the possibilities and potential implementation and timing. The buy decision was made within a week.

The way you phrase your questions and explore problems or opportunities affects the responses you receive. The POWNs acronym ensures that you cover what you need to know and what they may need to discover in the *Investigate* step.

To elevate the value you give the buyer and to differentiate yourself from your competition, explore the complete story of their POWNs; this will let you identify the details that allow you to collaborate with Them regarding your solution.

Get the Full Story with a Four-Point Investigation™

Imagine you have finished your investigation with a potential buyer and are committed to providing a recommendation or proposal. As you work on the recommendation and plan your next call, you realize you don't have all the information you really need. Sound familiar? This happens too often!

It's easy to get caught thinking "I have enough information and now it's time to tell them what I have or how I can help them." Premature recommendations, though, lead to extra follow-up activities and possible frustration for us and the buyer when the solution isn't accepted.

The framework for a complete *Investigation* presented in Figure 7–1 allows you to focus on key information you need to move forward in the sales process and close the sale.

Figure 7–1 Four-Point Investigation™

The graphic shows the framework of the four points. The points guide you through the questions that provide a full picture of the buyer's situation and allow you to identify the sales opportunity. Connecting your questions into a cohesive and logical approach that explores the *facts* of Today and

Tomorrow and the *emotional* and *logical* aspects of Risks and Rewards positions you as a collaborator.

The revolving center shows that an investigation can go in many directions. Where you begin your investigation doesn't matter. What does matter is that you connect and cover all four points. This flexible framework guides a relevant, natural, and value-filled investigation.

Often the buyer's first comments direct your conversation to begin at one point or another. They might start with discussing what they want or need. Or they may start talking about their frustrations Today or the vision they have for Tomorrow. They also might openly discuss the fears or Risks they are concerned about or the benefits or Rewards they seek from you, your product, or your service.

Following is a description of each of the points with thought-starter questions for you to build from. Tweak these questions to work in your situation:

Today questions ask for information about the buyer's current state. This is the back-story of what is happening now and explains how and why they are in their current situation. *Today* thought-starters include:

- "What type of budget process do you follow when deciding on _____?"

- "Help me understand some of the challenges you are facing with _____."

- "How does your decision process work?"

- "How well do your current systems integrate?"

- "What are your expectations from a _____ supplier?"

- "Please tell me about the _____ initiatives you are working on."

- "What makes your current supplier your preferred source?"

- "What solutions have you considered?"

- "Which issue is causing the biggest problem and why?"

- "What have you done in the past that worked well for _____?"

- "What has been your experience with _____?"

Tomorrow questions ask what the buyers want to happen or where they want and need to be. The gap between Tomorrow and Today is important because that is where your opportunity lies. If your solution can reduce/remove the gap between what is happening Today and where the buyer wants/needs to be Tomorrow, you have a viable prospect and potential sale. *Tomorrow* thought-starters include:

- "What are your future plans for _____?"

- "What are your priorities for _____?" *(fill in time frame)*

- "What capabilities do you wish _____ had that it currently doesn't have?"

- "From what you've already told me, how do you envision _____?"

- "What kind of strategy did you have in mind?"

- "What kind of help do you need?"

- "What is the ultimate intent for _____?"

- "How do you see yourself and others using _____?"

- "What are you trying to achieve?"

- "How would you like _____ to happen going forward?"

- "How will you measure ROI or results?"

- "What actions do you think we can take to improve the _____?"

- "What changes in the industry are causing the most trouble for you?"

Risk questions explore the potential downsides to moving to Tomorrow or staying in Today. Exploring the Risk of doing nothing is an effective way to identify the sense of urgency around the situation. These questions provide the buyer with powerful motivators to *do* something. *Risk* thought-starters include:

- "What types of liability are you exposed to if the situation remains unchanged?"

- "What will happen if you don't address _____?"

- "How would this change help you reduce risk for _____?"

- "What are the major issues you foresee from taking this action?"

- "What might be the consequences if we take no action?"

- "What does that mean to your business?"

- "If we start this, what *don't* you want to see happen?"

- "What are your concerns?"

- "Why do you feel this isn't going to work?"

- "What might be the risks in deciding on a solution now?"

- "What are the roadblocks to your preferred schedule?"

- "Tell me about your competitors' strengths? What risk does this pose to your company?"

Reward questions explore the benefits buyers are looking for when Tomorrow is reached and the potential benefits of them staying in Today. These questions help you understand the motivations that may drive the person to action and decision. *Reward* thought-starters include:

- "What can your company gain with the capabilities of this solution?"

- "What could you do with the time this solution will save you?"

- "How do you see this impacting your bottom line?"

- "With a decision to move forward, what type of advantage will you have over your competitors?"

- "What might you gain from having these newer _____?"

- "How much more efficient will your _____ be with these changes?"

- "How do you think this new solution will affect your marketability?"

- "How could this change help you meet your goals?"

- "How will your schedule improve if we make this change?"

- "What does success look like for you/your company?"

- "What do you want to enjoy once the solution is implemented?"

I've collected many additional thought-starter investigative questions for you on the www.conversationsthatsell.com website.

Covering all points in a Four-Point Investigation keeps you from moving the sale forward too soon and missing opportunities—for you and your buyer.

When a buyer called specifically to inquire about sales training, I acknowledged his request and asked permission to explore information at a higher level to give me context. Instead of jumping into a presentation of training solution offerings, I used the Four-Point Investigation framework to guide my questions.

First, I asked, and received, permission to question him further for information not directly related to the training he called about. (Getting permission is important: I didn't want him to feel I had hijacked the conversation.) I asked Today questions that focused him on his overall business and sales. I also asked Tomorrow questions that focused him on the goals and objectives most important to him personally. When those responses uncovered a more immediate business opportunity and the frustration and costs associated with it, I asked Risk questions about not addressing this opportunity before he invested in training, and Reward questions about what he would do with his time when a new sales leader was hired.

Using the four points as my guide expanded the conversation and uncovered underlying problems that were more pressing to my buyer and needed to be addressed first. What happened? We moved forward that day on the larger picture or problem—benchmarking and recruiting for a sales leader.

Although using the Four-Point Investigation framework is extremely helpful, it does not guarantee an easy *Investigation* with every buyer. Buyers generally have their comfort zone about what they are willing and ready to discuss. For this reason, knowing what to ask needs to be matched with *how* to ask questions they are willing and able to answer.

Ask Questions Buyers Want to Answer

While what you ask is important, *how* you ask open-ended questions is equally so. Used incorrectly, even open-ended questions can make an investigation seem like an interrogation. They can be leading, forced, narrow, product-focused, or irrelevant. Sellers can come off as militant when they drill questions directly at a prospect to gain the information that allows them to pitch their product without bringing the buyer into the collaborative process.

Instead of becoming an interrogator, you demonstrate your investigative professionalism when you incorporate the four I's into your questions: Make your questions Intentional, Intelligent, Interesting, and Indirect. Let's look at each of the I's in more detail.

Intentional Questions *Intentional questions* provide context to the buyer. They connect directly to the WiifT. I've seen sales pros launch right into their list of prepared questions, and I've watched their buyers give them a look that says, "What's this have to do with anything?" The buyer had no idea why these questions were being asked, what the seller's intent was, or if they should really answer the questions.

When you explain the intent of your questions, it gives the buyer perspective, which means the buyer can answer thoughtfully. The context of the line of questions gives clarity to the request, eases any discomfort, and opens a collaborative conversation.

I received a sales call some time ago in which the caller immediately asked, "So, what are you working on?" My reply? "Wow, that's broad. In what context?" He responded, "Whatever context you choose." Well, I was confused. I knew what this person was selling and wondered if I should answer based on that narrow interest or whether he was really trying to find out more.

So I turned it back to him and said, "What are you working on?" He responded, telling me in great detail what he was doing and about his services. After five minutes I knew where he really wanted the conversation to go— to his solution—and I wasn't interested.

Sharing intent, after a buyer has agreed to spend time with us, sounds like this:

> "We scheduled time to talk about your human resource needs. We've
> learned that understanding how HR fits into your overall company's goals

and objectives helps us narrow the information that will be useful to you, and we'll then be able to give you a more accurate picture of how we might help. The first questions are focused on that broader picture. Then we'll get more specific."

Now the conversation moves into your list of open-ended, relevant questions.

Intelligent Questions *Intelligent questions* draw from your experience and research. They differentiate you from the competition and most other sales pros. They are timely and help Them discover or clarify information or situations that are relevant. Buyers do not want their time wasted and asking them irrelevant and common questions can shut down your conversation and eliminate your potential sales opportunity. Your research about the market, value of your solutions, and this buyer all contribute to asking intelligent questions.

Here are a few tips on asking intelligent questions:

- Look at the company's website for recent news, the company's mission and vision, biographies of the people you will speak with, and financial results.

- Prepare a list of questions that will broaden the conversation beyond your product or service. For example, instead of asking, "What kind of an issue do you have with _____?" ask "In reviewing your company's website, I've noticed that your _____ is a strategic focus for next year. How does your _____ contribute to that focus?"

- Know the value your solution provides versus just the features. For example, if you sell a technology solution, a request for information about the impact of their current technology might be, "Please share with me how your technology service (*or* platform) impacts the daily operations of your facility."

- Know your industry and competitors. This allows you to ask questions such as, "How is the trend for _____ impacting your position or results?"

The questions asked during the *Investigate* step directly reflect your expertise on the topic of discussion. You demonstrate your brilliance—or lack thereof—during the investigation more than during the presentation of your solution!

✓ TIMELY TIP

A caution about Intelligent questions: Be careful not to use acronyms and terms that the buyer may not be familiar with. If they feel "dumb" or uninformed, it can shut them up rather than open up the conversation. No one likes a show-off. Gauge the buyer's expertise and knowledge and adjust your questions accordingly.

Interesting Questions *Interesting questions* are relevant to the situation and the person. When it's about Them, it's interesting to them and they will share more information and be more open to how you can help them. Every aspect of the sales process should be WiifT focused—What's in it for *Them?*—and this includes your questions!

Information you gather about the buyer's position, company, and situation can be used to ask questions that are relevant to the person. You don't typically ask the facility maintenance person the same questions in the same way as you would ask the facility administrator. The focus of their roles, their experiences, and their POWNs are different—and thus so should the questions.

Indirect Questions *Indirect questions* draw out the intent, emotions, and preferences of the buyer. To explain the importance of this type of question, I'll use an example of someone planning a vacation.

First, read the following questions:

- "How many people are in your family?"

- "What's your budget?"

- "Where do you want to go?"

- "Who will be traveling?"

- "What are your dates of travel?"

- "What airline do you prefer?"

- "Why do you want to stay in this location?"

Notice the tone of this series of questions. They begin with how, what, where, who. And at first they appear to be open-ended, yet they are really closed and direct. They lead directly to narrow specific information responses.

Now, read the following questions related to helping someone plan a vacation:

- "Tell me about the type of vacation you want to take."

- "What is your travel experience?"

- "What type of activities do you want to include in your trip?"

- "What is your budget?"

- "Who will be traveling with you?"

- "What places do you want to explore as options? Which do you want to stay away from?"

- "How many days do you have available for travel?"

- "What concerns do you have about traveling outside the country?"

- "What is one thing you want to experience?"

Notice how they ask for information, not just data. The responses to the second series of questions allow the vacation planner to collaboratively discuss options with the traveler.

Adjust Your Questions to the Tribal Type

Tribal Type preferences come into play during the *Investigate* step as well. When you speak their language, the questions and conversation are more rewarding.

Commanders and Achievers often prefer "thinking" words in their questions:

- "Please share with me your thoughts about _____."

- "What do you think is creating _____?"

  Reflectors and Expressers respond to "feeling" words in their questions.

- "How do you feel this will _____?"

- "How does your team prioritize _____?"

Years ago I was working with a group of high-level financial professionals. At the end of an activity I asked, "How do you feel that activity worked for you?" and directed the question to a woman in the group who stared blankly back at me. I waited for her response . . . five seconds, ten seconds, and then another participant said, "You asked a Commander a feeling question!"

I smiled and immediately restated the question, "Lisa, how do you *think* that activity worked for you?" She answered within moments.

Adjusting the questions to fit different Types isn't that difficult. Jeff Eigner, a Business Development Advisor, easily adjusted a question seeking a buyer's priorities to best resonate with the different Tribal Types:

- *Commander:* What does your analysis indicate are the top three issues facing you?

- *Reflector:* What has your team determined to be the top three issues?

- *Expresser:* How would you prioritize your top three issues?

- *Achiever:* What are the top three issues facing you?

Notice how the questions seek the same information, yet are phrased differently. Making your questions interesting means they are relevant and adjusted for Tribal Type preferences. In addition to word choice, the buyer's Tribal Type factors into what information they want to focus on.

The Commander and Achiever Tribal Types may be comfortable discussing problems and reviewing risks because they want to "fix" things. They want to address problems by tackling them head-on so they don't get in the way of success. This isn't always true for Expressers and Reflectors, who may want to avoid potential conflict.

Expressers and Achievers like to "dream" and are comfortable talking about opportunities. They are generally more open to being early adopters of ideas and solutions. Discussing hopes, dreams, and possibilities is energizing for them.

Different phrasing makes a profound impact on how easy your questions are to answer. If you speak with multiple decision makers, this personal example may sound familiar.

Many years ago when my husband, Jon, and I started working with our financial advisor, Mike Haubrich, he asked us, "What are your dreams for the future?" My husband, a Commander/Reflector, was confused: What did this have to do with our money? Wasn't Mike a *financial* advisor? Why would discussing our dreams for the future play into a review of our portfolio? He wanted Mike to narrow that question down into a time frame with more concrete specifics.

On the other hand, I am an Achiever/Expresser and I loved the question. I wanted to talk about the vacation home I hoped we would have, funding the kids' college education, and the plans for expanding my business. I was frustrated that Jon didn't want to discuss the wonderful opportunities for our careers, finances, and family.

Jon also is very comfortable exploring and focusing on potential risks and problems, while I quickly sort through risks and minimize them, focusing more on the potential rewards. Mike has his hands full working with us, allowing each of us to explore our combined and individual POWNs in ways that are interesting to each of us.'

Asking great questions is a very important action in the *Investigate* step, and we've just covered the whats and hows of asking these questions. Prepare to make your questions productive and then pair the great questions with Actions 2, 3, and 4 of the *Investigate* step to be an investigator rather than an interrogator.

ACTION 2: LISTEN ACTIVELY

Active listening is an action. It's something you do; it is not a passive endeavor. Active listening means you are involved, engaged, and present during the conversation. It confirms that they are the focus of the conversation.

Your ability and willingness to listen demonstrates that you are engaged with them and care about the information the buyer is sharing. To listen actively:

- *Pay attention.* Use eye contact, eliminate distractions, and avoid multitasking.

- *Respond to what is being said with sounds and movement.* Verbal responses are especially necessary in telephone conversations.

- *Focus on the person and watch for signals that show you their intent and emotion.* These signals may include body language, tone, and pace.

- *Remain open to the responses and hear their full answer before judging or responding.*

- *Take notes.* Not only do notes serve as a reference later, making the notes slows your mind down in the moment so you listen better.

Listening actively allows us to converse and collaborate through the *Investigate* step. It keeps the conversation flowing smoothly. The actual skill of listening isn't usually the problem, though. It's more often the discipline and execution of talking less so that we can listen better. Often a "talking trigger," something that makes you talk more than you should or need to, takes over. These triggers can be:

- Nervousness.

- Lack of confidence.

- The desire or need to prove ourselves.

- Uncertainty as to where to go next in the conversation.

- The desire to convince or talk someone into something.

- Not having been trained to listen!

To listen more, prepare for your conversations. (Yes, because preparation is key to being most effective and to eliminating the habits that kill sales, I'm going to discuss preparation over and over again.) Identify your talking trigger and eliminate it with proper Preparation.

If your trigger is nervousness when the person doesn't respond to questions or is clearly in a hurry, prepare the list of questions you'd like answered—and then prepare a shorter list in case there isn't enough time to ask them all. Start with the questions on the short list—and be prepared to ask for the decision to schedule the next meeting.

Sometimes, just forcing yourself to listen rather than talk—even if it's to ask great questions—works well. Years ago, a client, Rick, referred me to a prospect and I was able to easily schedule the appointment using Rick as the connection. The one-hour telephone sales call focused on the buyer. I asked questions that I had prepared and forced myself to listen as I took notes and made verbal sounds of paying attention—*uh huh, oh,* and *hmmm.*

I paraphrased his responses and when he had an interruption and needed to end the call early, I asked to speak with him again, and he agreed. I hung up and then thought, "Oh, that was a waste of time. I never got a chance to explain anything to him and he has no idea what I do or how I can help him." The following day, Rick asked me how my call went. As I was about to share with him my concerns about not getting a chance to really converse, he blurted out, "Well, whatever you did he thought you were brilliant!"

When you actively listen and focus all your attention on the buyer—and if you don't let your triggers set your mouth in motion—your buyer will think *you* are brilliant and will want to continue the conversation.

Your ability, skill, and attitude toward listening are equally as important as asking the right questions. The combination of asking for the right information, hearing what they tell you, and then presenting a solution that addresses their POWNs is what wins sales.

ACTION 3: ASK FOLLOW-UP QUESTIONS

To keep the conversation collaborative between you and the buyer, use follow-up questions in your *Investigation*. After asking prepared questions, seek further clarification or information about the buyer's response in order to further explore their POWNs. Use follow-up questions to ask for more information about specifics, detail, and intent.

Follow-up questions sound like this:

- "That's interesting. Please tell me more about _____."

- "I understand that _____ is your priority this year. How does that impact _____?"

- "I've heard similar things from other buyers. How do *you* see _____?"

- "Please explain your specific problem in more detail."

Your follow-up questions demonstrate how well you are listening to more than the words the buyer is sharing; they showcase your expertise and continue to prove the value you can provide.

ACTION 4: PARAPHRASE WHAT THE BUYER HAS STATED

"Paraphrasing is powerful," I explain to my course participants. Knowing that you will paraphrase—words and intent—keeps you focused, shows buyers you have heard them, and allows them to hear back a summary of their own messages. After they hear your paraphrase, it's not uncommon for the buyer to clarify or explain certain points, which is helpful for both of you.

TIMELY TIP

Paraphrasing is not word-for-word repeating of what the buyer shared with you; that is parroting. Instead, summarize the intent and "story" that you heard in your own words.

* * *

The *Investigate* step of the WIIFT sales system allows your buyer to clarify and discover their POWNs, and helps you identify their sense of urgency as well as their openness to reviewing solutions with you.

To determine if it's time to move to the next step of the WIIFT system, summarize the information you have compiled and then complete the last Action for *Investigate*, which includes qualifying your buyer.

ACTION 5: QUALIFY AND
CONFIRM YOUR OPPORTUNITY

Qualify and confirm that They want to discuss a solution before moving on. Qualify that the buyer is the right person to advance the sale with, that they have the budget, and that they want to *do* something to address their POWNs. Then confirm that you have understood their situation correctly and that they are open to discussing a solution with you. The following questions qualify and confirm:

• "Before we go on, who else should be included in our conversation?"

• "What is the budget you have for this?"

• "What's your timing for looking at solutions?"

TIMELY TIP

It's easy to assume that someone who has shared information with you must want to act on that information. Not true! Before investing time and effort in collaborating about recommendations, confirm that they are open to a solution—and their timing. It will help you prioritize where to spend your time and energy.

A complete Investigation may look cumbersome and lengthy. Yet it doesn't need to be. Depending on what you sell, three or four questions may be all you need to discover POWNs, qualify, and move forward. Other sales cycles may include several calls or visits to *Investigate*.

GROUP INVESTIGATIONS

Extracting information from a group provides additional challenges. You can imagine some of the underlying dynamics that impact an open discussion of POWNs. Getting individuals to contribute information in front of their spouses, colleagues, and managers takes extra effort.

To increase your probability of gathering good information in a group setting:

- Send questions to the group in advance of your conversation.

- During the conversation, poll the group or ask each person for a response.

- Pay attention to body language to spot those who may have something to say but are not speaking up.

- Tell the group they have a certain period of time to send in more detailed responses after the conversation—give a full day if possible, or at least until the day's end.

- Ask for information in different ways to resonate with the different Tribal Types.

- If one person is dominating the discussion, ask follow-up questions to others using their name, "Thank you, Anne. That was very helpful. Steve, what can you add to the information Anne shared?"

* * *

Each buyer situation is unique. Your preparation and ability to *Investigate* POWNs with your buyer in different ways earns you the right to advance your sales conversation to the *Facilitate* step.

QUICK TIPS TO INVESTIGATE POWNs™

- Ask relevant, open-ended questions. Identify the buyer's POWNs and ensure your questions are intentional, intelligent, interesting, and indirect.

- Use the Four-Point Investigation framework to ensure you are asking for the information that opens sales opportunities. Ask for information about Today and Tomorrow, about Risk and Reward.

- Use the thought-starter questions throughout this chapter to create a list of between ten and fifteen questions that you want to incorporate into your investigations.

- Adjust your questions for the Tribal Type. Use "thinking" words in the questions for Commanders and Achievers and "feeling" words for Expressers and Reflectors.

- Listen actively. Nod your head, verbalize that you hear the buyer, and focus on their responses.

- Pay attention to your listening habits. Determine if they are effective and, if not, set a goal to make incremental changes to listen more.

- Ask follow-up questions. Clarify the buyer's responses and seek more information.

- Paraphrase what the buyer has stated. Summarize, don't parrot back. Capture the emotions as well as the facts.

- Qualify the buyer before moving to the *Facilitate* step or recommending a solution. Ask about the decision-making process and timing, and determine what other people should be included in the conversation.

CHAPTER 8

Facilitate, Part I: Create Collaborative Solution Presentations Focused on the Buyer

"Everything should be made as simple as possible, but not simpler."
—ALBERT EINSTEIN, physicist

To facilitate means to make it easier, or less difficult, for something to be accomplished—which is exactly what we need to do for our buyers; make it easy for them to see how our solution matters to *Them*. You help Them easily see how your solution connects to their specific POWNs with the *Facilitate* step. Facilitating is not as much show and tell as it is collaborate and sell. It's your opportunity to demonstrate your solution and expertise.

Buyers need an easy way to learn about your solution so they can decide if it has value to them and determine whether they will spend more time with you, move forward in the sales process, and ultimately, make the purchase. They need you to value their time and energy and will find *you* valuable when you collaboratively discuss how your solution specifically addresses *their* POWNs. Providing information that is timely and relevant to the buyer keeps the conversation collaborative and focused on Them.

Your goal is to make it easy for them to:

- Identify the value they will receive.

- Sell it to someone else—their spouse, manager, or team.

- Make a decision.

- Quickly receive or implement the solution.

FIVE ACTIONS THAT MAKE IT EASY FOR BUYERS TO CONNECT TO YOUR SOLUTION

Too little information shared or too much information not directly connected to their POWNs quickly kills your sales opportunity. The five Actions in *Facilitate* guide you through a collaborative presentation and discussion of your solution that keeps the opportunity alive:

1. Explain your solution with Whats to WiifTs.

2. Include others in the presentation and ask for feedback.

3. Provide proof to support your solution.

4. Present costs followed by value.

5. Ask for and work through objections with Stop, Drop, and Roll.

This chapter covers the first four Actions for a productive, collaborative recommendation of your solutions. The final Action of working through objections, concerns, and questions is so important that it has its own chapter, Chapter 9.

The first four *Facilitate* Actions work in all types of solution presentation situations: one on one, group sales, telephone sales, webinars, formal presentations, and team presentations.

The *Facilitate* step begins the process of discussing and setting expectations about your solution and your ongoing relationship.

ACTION 1: EXPLAIN YOUR SOLUTION BY CONNECTING WHATS TO WIIFTS

Your solution presentation is more powerful when you connect the information about your solution to what you learned in the *Investigate* step, that is, when you connect your solution to their specific POWNs. This connection makes the information both relevant and valuable for Them!

Begin by explaining *what* your solution has or *what* it does for them and then connect those details to the benefits or *What's in it for Them.* I call these "Whats to WiifTs." Whats to WiifTs keep your buyers from having to make the feature-to-benefit connection themselves and ensures that they understand the value of your solution. If you only present features of your solution, buyers can get distracted, become indifferent, or start feeling that they are being sold to.

What + WiifT = Value

Don't assume the value for Them is obvious just because you have described what your solution has or does. It takes energy and effort to make these connections, so *we* need to make it easy for the buyers and make the connection for Them. Busy buyers won't necessarily make the connection or that they will sort through the information to specifically identify the value they will receive from your solution.

"Whats to WiifTs" sound like this:

- "Our solution includes 24/7 support so that you never have a delay in accessing the help system."

- "The solution provides real-time data reporting that gives your team current information when troubleshooting customer issues."

State What Your Solution Has or Does
The Whats are the features and attributes of your solution. They describe your product or service. For example, "experts on staff," "thirty-day turn-

around," "leather seats," "twenty-four-hour support," "competitive pricing," "local representation," and "12-gauge steel" are all Whats.

The details of the Whats of your solution (the features) are readily available in sales materials, on your website, and shared in training sessions. The problem typically isn't knowing enough Whats; it's relating the correct Whats to each buyer. The most relevant Whats to discuss are those that directly address the buyer's POWNs.

For example, if you sell home improvement services and the buyer's POWNs are an updated kitchen, the relevant Whats to discuss are your ability to remodel a kitchen, not details about how good your company is at creating a spa-like master bedroom or installing a fence.

Answer "So What?" to Connect the What to the WiifT

Connect the Whats of your solution to their POWNs to demonstrate that you heard Them in the *Investigate* step. Make it a seamless connection by using a connecting phrase that includes the words "you" or "your." This phrase becomes a spotlight illuminating the person, the value, or the benefits. It sends the message, "Hey, pay attention, this is about you!"

To identify relevant WiifTs, imagine that as each What is presented, the buyer is thinking "So what?" or "So what does this have to do with me?" To answer the "So what?" question, connect a relevant WiifT to the What to focus Them on what is important:

- Our wireless timekeeping systems are run by GPS, allowing *you* to always have accurate time so that *your records are legally compliant.*

- We will develop a custom hiring process that *provides your company with a streamlined and cost-effective process.*

- Our customer service department is open 24/7, *so you will never have to wait* to contact us if you need help

- The weather station provides constant monitoring of the environment so you can make adjustments within minutes, *saving your crops from damage.*

- The annual financial review includes a comprehensive report of the transactions of your investment accounts, which will *save you time* during year-end tax preparation.

Other connecting phrases you can use include:

- For **your** situation . . .

- What this means for **you** . . .

- So **you** will be able to . . . *or*, So that **you** . . .

- This allows **you** to . . . *or*, This allows **your** team to . . .

- In **your** situation this means that . . .

You will find the connection phrases that sound and feel right to you as you make Whats to WiifTs connections. Not only does personalizing your phrases keep you from sounding phony and rehearsed, it allows you to vary the way you explain the information throughout your conversation.

Whats to WiifTs is an easy concept, but we need to use our knowledge skillfully to connect the *right* WiifTs. In your preparation, identify relevant WiifTs by specifically identifying how your solution:

- Solves their problems.

- Captures opportunities for them.

- Fills their wants and needs.

- Ties into each buyer's specific situation.

Your answers will allow you to share powerful, relevant WiifT statements for different buying situations.

ACTION 2: INCLUDE OTHERS IN THE PRESENTATION AND ASK FOR FEEDBACK

Although the topic of discussion is now your product or service, it's still not all about you; it's about you *and* Them. A focus on this "we" dynamic continues to engage your buyer in the conversation and differentiates you from your competition. They remain engaged when you include Them as you facilitate the presentation of your solution. A solution presentation is not necessarily a stand-up presentation, it's however you first communicate the information about your solution.

Put yourself in the mode of buyer and suppose you decide to purchase a new sofa. The furniture showroom seller does a great job of investigating your POWNs and points to your sofa options. She then leads you to the service counter and asks "Which sofa do you think will best suit you?"

How would you feel? Would you be ready to select your sofa and make the purchase? Probably not.

You weren't involved in the review of your options, allowed to sit on the sofas to determine how they fit you, or to compare different sofas. You were robbed of the opportunity to select the right one for you or to start mentally picturing one in your home.

What if, instead, the seller followed their investigation with:

> "From what you told me, comfort and color are the two most important considerations for you. What else is important to you? *(Pause for response.)* Let's look at your options, give you time to sit and recline in different sofas, and when you find the sofa that feels right, we'll look at color options. Most of our pieces can be custom ordered in dozens of fabrics. Let's start over here."

Then you spend time sitting on sofas, reviewing the different options, and selecting a fabric while continuing your conversation with the seller about what you like and don't like about the sofas you've been shown.

The seller says: "It looks like we have found the right fit for comfort and the color that is right for your room. What questions or concerns do you have about that sofa?"

How would you feel now? Would you be ready to continue the conversation and explore whether this is the right sofa for you?

The chances are much higher that you would continue, aren't they?

It's the same with your buyers. They don't want to be passive subjects when reviewing your solution and its fit to their POWNs—they want to get their hands (and minds) on it!

When buyers are passive, they can flip into the mode of the discriminating buyer: "I tell you what I want, and then sit back and judge or dismiss your suggestions or solution." When they are not a part of the solution, it is easier for them to be a detached judge and jury.

Collaboratively Involve Your Buyer

How then do we involve our buyers when presenting information about our solution? We engage Them collaboratively with healthy doses of inclusion.

First, invite Them to participate in this part of the conversation. "Let's explore how our solution addresses what we just discussed." With this set-up of inclusion, you set the expectation that they are involved in the presentation and discussion of your solution. Involve them mentally and physically whether your conversation is face-to-face, on the telephone, or in a group selling situation.

You can engage their *minds* with:

- *Stories.* Explain how your solution addresses their POWNs or how it has solved POWNs for other people. These stories are helpful if you provide a service or a physical product. Give them background, action, and outcome. Stories work in two ways. Current customers are recognized for their wise decision in how they addressed their POWNs and new buyers hear about real situations and begin to picture themselves enjoying the same outcome.

- *Best practices.* Buyers want to know what others are doing that works well. Explain how-to's and specifics of not only your solution's results, but how other buyers have implemented the solution and other best practices around it.

You can engage their *hands* and *senses* with:

- *Hands-on items.* Put something in their hands—paper, the mouse, or the product whenever possible. If you don't have a physical product, involve their hands by having them click on Web pages or holding a document.

- *Prototypes and samples.* In some industries, a prototype can be made to show what it would look, sound, or work like. Add their company logo or name in printed materials or to slides to begin their thoughts of ownership. Getting people to touch and try works!

- *Visual aids.* PowerPoints, written materials, screen sharing, and webinars are all powerful tools to help the buyer see your solution and the

WiifT. Use diagrams and metaphoric imagery to make a point, draw a correlation, and show the potential benefits. The key is to turn these aids into tools that help make it about Them and less about you; use them to demonstrate capabilities of what you have and what it can do for Them.

Determine the viable inclusion ideas for your solution and consistently ask feedback questions throughout the presentation—one of the easiest ways to keep Them involved.

Ask Feedback Questions

As you share Whats to WiifTs about your solution, regularly seek the buyer's viewpoint, opinions, and feelings about the fit of the solution to their POWNs or their expectations with feedback questions.

Tap into their experiences and expertise to discover and discuss the benefits and challenges of your solution, explore their opinion, and collaborate on how to implement what you offer. Educated buyers want to be acknowledged for their knowledge.

Responses to feedback questions often reward you with additional information about the buyer's intent, sense of urgency, and POWNs. This information provides you additional insight into their motivators and the impact of emotional influences.

Of course it's possible that asking for feedback could produce negative information or unrealistic expectations. That's okay though, because you can use this as an opportunity to circle back in WIIFT to further explore or clarify their POWNs.

Feedback questions keep Them engaged, save time, identify objections and concerns early, and redirect the conversation back to the *Investigate* step if the solution is not a fit.

The following examples of feedback questions encourage your buyer to share useful information:

- "How does this match up with what you were considering?"

- "How do you see this moving you toward where you want to be?"

- "What is the best part of what we have discussed?"

- "Where do you see this fitting in with your priorities?"

Listen to their initial feedback and then clarify, if necessary, with additional follow-up questions:

- "That's interesting. Tell me more."

- "You make a good point. How else can you see this working?"

- "What other ideas do you have?"

- "What do you think the reaction of others will be?"

- "Tell me what you think about _____."

Buyers begin to sell themselves as they collaboratively discuss possibilities and their feedback. Your final solution, implementation, delivery schedule, and terms are often better when developed collaboratively.

Tap into Team Expertise

Many sales are not closed with just one seller and one buyer. Involve your team or buyer's teams when necessary to speed up the sales process. Include *your* team members whenever possible to:

1. Bring additional expertise to the discussion.

2. Demonstrate the strength or depth of expertise within your company.

3. Match Tribal Type needs more strongly.

4. Give more opportunity for individual engagement if you are with a group of buyers.

Include the *buyer's team* early in the conversation or sales process when possible to secure buy-in more quickly, clarify POWNs, and provide a different viewpoint.

Involving the buyer and engaging Them throughout the conversation produces high dividends. They pay closer attention, participate at higher levels, identify a higher perceived value, and will be more inclined to make a buying decision. It keeps Them from sitting back and judging you and your solution.

ACTION 3: PROVIDE PROOF TO
SUPPORT YOUR SOLUTION

"Prove" is the umbrella over the entire WIIFT system, as shown in Figure 8–1. "Proving" shelters you from many common objections and lack of trust issues that can stall your sale. Providing proof never ends in the selling process; your genuineness, expertise, intentions, and value are constantly evaluated!

Figure 8–1   WIIFT

Proof is also a factor in your success in the *Facilitate* step of WIIFT. It's *the* time to make sure the proof and evidence are enough for that buyer.

Provide proof to support your solution by proving:

- *Who you are.* Every action you take or word you say—or don't take or say—proves something about your character, expertise, and your level of professionalism. This proof shows throughout the entire conversation and, more importantly, throughout the entire relationship.

- *The value your solution provides.* Providing proof for your solution is crucial during the *Facilitate* step. Include the following proof sources when sharing information about your solution: metrics, testimonials and references, hands-on demos, validated third-party research, examples from experiences with other buyers, and guarantees/warranties.

The key to proving is providing the *right* proof and evidence for the person and situation. To help you incorporate relevant proof information, use your understanding of Tribal Type customs.

- *Commanders* want primary source research, validated proof, metrics, fact sheets, and testimonials that include analysis.

- *Reflectors* need details, guarantees, and case studies to know the why and how.

- *Expressers* like personal testimonials, second opinions, references, and your confidence.

- *Achievers* want to know the bottom-line output, metrics of outcomes, and time considerations, and they want to be able to contact high-profile references.

Continuous proof is necessary in the *Facilitate* step and throughout the conversation. Why? Can you think of a relationship where once you've proven yourself you never had to again? Not many of us can. Without proof it is difficult to move forward in your sales conversation.

ACTION 4: PRESENT COSTS FOLLOWED BY VALUE

Presenting your solution collaboratively might be the easiest part of the *Facilitate* step. But at some point in facilitating your solution, it's time to talk cost. And often this is when the conversation becomes uncomfortable. Why? I believe it is uncomfortable for sellers if:

1. They personally don't see the value justification of what they are offering for the cost.

2. The buyer has not articulated that they see value in the solution—yet.

3. Budgets haven't been discussed, so the seller has assumptions about what the buyer is willing or able to pay.

Working through WIIFT sequentially eliminates these barriers to a productive and value-filled discussion of the costs. Place your cost discussion *after* you've collaborated with the buyer and identified the most viable solution. Then present the costs followed by value (WiifT).

Explore the Real Costs to Your Solution

Costs are not just about money; the real costs for the buyer purchasing your solution are more complex. There are financial costs, time costs, opportunity costs, change costs, relationships costs, and more. Sometimes the non-monetary costs are the biggest barrier to the sale moving forward. Setting proper expectations for *all* the costs means there are no surprises for the buyer after the sale.

Connect the Cost to Value

Imagine that the last words spoken or written during any part of the sales conversation hang in the air for buyers to look at, analyze, and focus on. When the final words are about cost, that's what the buyer will focus on. Instead, let those hanging words be about the value—the WiifT.

Connecting cost to value is the same as translating Whats to WiifTs. After all, isn't the cost just another What or feature of your solution?

When presented with the costs, the buyer may be thinking, "Why should we incur these costs? What's in it for me?" Answer the Why with the WiifT response to what they really receive: their POWNs addressed. The buyer isn't just getting a solution. They're getting the value or benefits of that solution: "By buying the paper clips and storage bins you get an uncluttered office." "This model not only will transport you safely and dependably, its thirty-eight miles per gallon saves you money." "This custom-made suit flatters your figure and you'll feel confident as you present at the board meeting."

Another consideration when talking cost is the language you use. Terms such as expense, price, and investment have different connotations. The word you use will resonate differently with different buyers. While "investment" might not fit every situation, helping your buyers translate price into value that addresses their POWNs makes any cost an investment.

No matter what you call the financial payment for your product or service, delivering the information is easier, and perceived value increases, when you connect it to value and how their POWNs are addressed:

- "The cost of the sofa is $1,250, and for that you have a beautiful piece of furniture that fits your tall family comfortably and the custom fabric coordinates with your existing décor, so you won't have to repaint the walls."

- "The IT project we have agreed on is $87,900 for all three phases of development. With this investment, your time frame will be met with few time resources used from your team, so they can remain focused on the year-end processing project."

Connect the value for Them with cost Whats to WiifTs in verbal and written recommendations or proposals.

Traps to Avoid When Talking Cost

When talking costs, our words, actions, and assumptions may send messages we don't intend. These become traps that confuse the value we are trying to communicate.

Things not to say: Every word you use in your cost discussion sends a message to the buyer. Your words can set up price haggling or demonstrate you lack confidence in your solution. Avoid phrases such as:

- "The price is usually _____."

- "This is our _____ *(usual, quoted, regular, best, list, basic)* price."

- "If you're going to buy this much, I can try to work my manager for a better deal."

- "Tell me where I need to be."

- "What do I have to do to get your business?"

- "Am I in the ballpark?"

- "Our price is lower than anyone else's." (They may want to verify this claim.)

Body language to avoid: Your body language is read carefully by your buyer. Ensure you are not averting your eyes, crossing your arms, positioning your body away from Them, or hesitating before talking about the costs. Avoid less subtle actions such as positioning yourself as hopeless, helpless, or not part of the solution by siding with the buyer and setting up a we/they with your manager or company. "I would do this, but they don't allow it" is not the way to achieve the Win[3].

Assumptions you shouldn't make: Be careful that you do not impose your personal belief in what someone else is willing to pay or do when it comes to time or change costs. If you wouldn't invest two days of time in getting something done, that doesn't mean that the buyer wouldn't. Don't make assumptions about what they are willing and able to pay based on their position, industry, or personal considerations. There are many wealthy business owners who always look for huge discounts and many poor consumers who will fork over $50 for a tube of lipstick.

TIMELY TIP

Your personal beliefs about costs significantly impact the cost discussion. If you don't believe your solution is worth the cost, neither will your buyer. To build your belief, identify the Whats to WiifTs before having the buyer conversation. List the Whats on a piece of paper and ask yourself multiple "So Whats?" to identify the value associated with each What. This preparation will boost your confidence and lead to less cost discounting and fewer objections.

FACILITATING A GROUP SALES CONVERSATION

Facilitating a collaborative and inclusive solution discussion is more complex in group situations. Involving everyone in a group takes preparation and flexibility in the moment. To involve the group, vary the way you *Facilitate* this part of the sales conversation:

- *Ask different types of feedback questions.* Allow the individuals to provide the feedback in writing either before or after your meeting.

- *Involve everyone physically and mentally* with stories, visual aids, and sharing samples and documents with each person.

- *Facilitate group discovery and clarity.* Ask different people for feedback, to contribute an idea, to use markers or the keyboard, or to take notes on a handout.

- *Provide different types of proof.* This will appeal to the different Tribal Types in the group.

WHAT TO DO WHEN YOUR SOLUTION DOESN'T FIT

What do you do if your buyers are not engaged or don't want to be included in discussing options? What do you do when you find that their feedback indicates they do not see value or think your solution will help with their POWNs? Or, when you realize that what you offer isn't the right solution for Them?

If you discover your solution doesn't fit, let Them know as early as possible to achieve a different type of Win[3]. Everyone wins when you stop trying to fit a round peg into a square hole. *You* win when you are upfront and honest, *your* company is saved from a dissatisfied customer, and *the customer* will appreciate your up-front approach and honesty. Everyone saves a lot of time and energy, and you can focus on more probable business opportunities. Identifying a misfit can also earn you more than a sale—it can earn you a positive reputation and new sales opportunities.

In a meeting with a national staffing company leader of training, we explored their POWNs and I knew we would not be the best fit to meet their timing needs. I told the leader so and then shared the name of a local consultant who would be perfect. The leader put his hands on his chair arms and said, "I want my people to do what you just did!" While I didn't get his business that day, over the next three months he did send me two referrals. Not a bad outcome for honesty.

If you aren't quite sure if there is a fit, then circle back to the *Investigate* step or work through these concerns with Stop, Drop, and Roll—the final Action of the *Facilitate* step, which we will cover in Chapter 9.

* * *

Prepare to connect the Whats to the WiifTs, involve Them, prove your information, and talk costs. You will find this investment of time and effort well worth it because the sale moves along more quickly when the buyer feels they are part of the solution outcome.

Powerful presentations that engage, include, and demonstrate value are the perfect setup to boost acceptance to your solution.

QUICK TIPS TO FACILITATE THE
PRESENTATION OF YOUR SOLUTION

- Connect your solution to the value the buyer receives using Whats to WiifTs.

- Prepare to include your buyer in different ways when discussing your solution. Involve Them mentally and physically by telling stories, sharing best practices, offering hands-on items, showing prototypes and samples, and asking feedback questions. Involve their senses whenever possible.

- Connect value to the cost information using Whats to WiifTs.

- Incorporate your buyer's Tribal Type customs into the types of proof and WiifTs you share.

- For groups, use a variety of inclusion strategies and proof points to engage and involve everyone.

CHAPTER 9

Facilitate, Part II: Work Through Objections

*"When solving problems, dig at the roots
instead of just hacking at the leaves."*
—ANTHONY J. D'ANGELO, **author of** *The College Blue Book*

You're in a conversation with a buyer and it's going well. You've *Initiated* a positive connection and engaged in a productive *Investigation* where you discovered his POWNs. You've *Facilitated* a collaborative presentation of your solution and he agrees your solution will work. *But...* now there is an objection or a question.

What's your reaction to the objection or question? Most people react with fight or flight.

Fight is to start bombarding the buyer with more information to try and talk them into your way of thinking. *Flight* is to avoid or minimize the objection, concern, or question.

Neither of these reactions advances the sale, trust, collaboration, or relationship.

Your own reaction to the objection and the buyer's prior sales purchasing experiences both come into play at this time. The buyer may fear you will ignore the objection and both of you may anticipate a confrontation over price or another issue.

Objections in the sales conversation are often nothing more than problems to be solved. When objections are uncovered, it doesn't have to become an "us or them" situation; in collaborative selling with a WiifT focus, we work through objections *with* our buyers.

In collaborative selling, we solve the problem together. Even more valuable than problem solving, though, is problem *re*solving. The difference in solution and resolution is significant. Problem solution identifies an answer for today. Problem resolution seeks a long-term solution or permanent fix.

If pricing is the objection, for example, providing a discount may solve the problem and close the sale today, but what happens for future purchases? Will the buyer expect the same discount or want more? A *re*solution could be scheduling repeat deliveries to earn a discount, different payment terms, or adjusting the solution to fit within the price they are willing or able to pay. As a long-term resolution, this elevates your value and assures you reach a Win^3.

How, then, do you collaborate with Them for a mutual, problem-resolving outcome? By facilitating Them *through* the objection or concern.

ACTION 5: ASK FOR AND WORK THROUGH OBJECTIONS WITH STOP, DROP, AND ROLL™

The final Action in the *Facilitate* step of WIIFT is to ask for and work through objections with a strategy called Stop, Drop, and Roll, the topic of this chapter. As you work through Facilitating the match of your solution to the buyer's POWNs, it's natural that this is when the buyer will think of and express questions . . . and objections. And believe it or not, that's a *good* thing.

We can't work through objections if we don't know about them. Give your buyers the opportunity to discuss them by asking if they have any objections, concerns, or questions.

Asking for objections may seem like we're giving buyers an opportunity to slow down or stop the sale. Maybe you've been taught to push forward in the sale and hope that objections don't arise, or perhaps you've had training in how to "handle" objections.

Those approaches don't work well in building loyal customers. Ignoring or "handling" an objection doesn't make it go away; it just buries it temporarily. The objection will surface again—usually when you aren't expecting it. Instead, buyers want you to *resolve* their objection quickly, productively, and with a focus on Them.

To set the stage for collaboration when an objection is voiced, respond with Stop, Drop, and Roll (see Figure 9–1).

Why "Stop, Drop, and Roll?" The term represents an important safety tip taught in many schools: if your clothes are on fire, stop, drop (to the ground), and roll to extinguish the flames. Though we aren't literally on fire when we hear an objection, concern, or question, the conversation may get heated and seem as if we are.

Figure 9–1 Stop, Drop, and Roll™

Stop, Drop, and Roll is a strategy for working *through* objections or questions:

Stop what you are doing, saying, and thinking to pay attention to the buyer. Listen to their tone, observe their body language, and pay attention to their words. This pause allows you to take a breath and engage your mind before your mouth.

Drop your defenses, agenda, assumptions, and ego before saying anything.

Roll forward by working as a problem resolver with Them using the three A's as your guide: *Acknowledge* the objection; *Ask* clarifying questions; and *Answer* collaboratively.

Acknowledge the Objection

Acknowledge that you hear the objection and demonstrate you will not fight or flee. Acknowledgment sends the buyer the message that they have been heard, that you are open to what they have to say, and that you truly want to understand their objection.

Acknowledgment sounds like this:

- "I understand that the timing of implementation doesn't work for you."

- "What I hear you saying is that there are questions about the reliability of our solution."

Notice that the acknowledgment phrases focus on the fact that you *hear* their concern or objection, not necessarily that you *agree* with them. Agreeing with their objection can seem condescending, as if you are pacifying them, or faking it. It can also appear as if you are working against your company, which doesn't support the Win^3 focus.

There are many ways to begin your Acknowledgment. To keep it from sounding scripted, use phrases that are comfortable for you and that resonate with your buyer's Tribal Type, such as:

- "I appreciate knowing or hearing _____."

- "Thank you for sharing that _____."

- "What I hear you saying is _____."

- "Uh-huh, or Okay, _____."

- "I can understand that _____."

- "It sounds like _____."

- "If I understand you correctly, _____."

Be careful that your Acknowledgment does not "name" their emotion, such as: "I understand your *frustration* . . ." or "I hear that you are *afraid* that . . ." If they haven't named their emotion, neither should you. If you name the wrong emotion, you create a new objection. If you tell the buyer you understand they are afraid, or confused, or frustrated and that is not their emotion, they might then want to address that topic instead of the real one. Instead, use "I understand that you are saying _____" or "I hear that you _____," and then paraphrase the objection.

Ask Clarifying Questions

After acknowledging that you hear the buyer, clarify that you have heard the root objection or concern. This clarification actually may speed up the process of resolution. As American author and magazine editor Dorothea Brande said, "A problem clearly stated is a problem half solved." That's why we need to stop and ask a question to ensure we are addressing the right problem.

Ask an open-ended question to draw out more information and clarify the objection or concern. Seeking clarity saves you time and energy from trying to solve the wrong problem.

The clarifying question should be indirect, nondefensive, and designed to seek understanding and more information. Gaps in information often create concerns and objections. As buyers clarify the objection or concern they often talk themselves through it, removing the objection before it becomes necessary for you to offer price discounting, concessions, or changes to the solution or terms.

Segue from your Acknowledgment to Asking a clarifying question with phrases such as:

- "So that I can determine what can be done, ..."

- "Let's see how we might look at this together. Please tell me more about _____."

- "I'd like to explore that further . . . ."

Then use questions or phrases that request more information, like the thought-starters that follow:

- "What makes the timing of delivery challenging for you?"

- "Help me understand more about your feelings/thoughts that your resources will be underutilized."

- "How do you see this getting in the way?"

Listen to their response, paraphrase, and, if necessary, ask another clarification question.

A caution about your clarification questions: Be aware that initially asking the question, "Why?" may cause a defensive reaction. Though we need to understand where the objection is coming from, "Why?" can put the person on the defensive and make it harder for us to collaborate with Them. Instead, ask: "How does _____?" or "What makes _____?" to start.

Answer Collaboratively

After the buyer clarifies their objection or question, you can determine which way to Roll in WIIFT—back to the *Investigate* step to further explore POWNs or back to the earlier Actions in the *Facilitate* step to discuss more WiifTs. You may also find you have addressed the objection through the clarifying questions and can simply Roll forward to *Then Consolidate.*

Since a collaborative approach to objections might be a new approach—and a welcome one—for your buyer, set the collaborative expectation by letting the buyer know that you want to work *with* Them to identify the best resolution. Give them hope that their objection can be resolved with collaborative Answers like:

- "I can see how this is a concern for you. A client of mine had the same reaction last month. Then we worked together to identify a solution that worked well for them. Would you like to see what we can do to explore additional options?"

- "Thank you for explaining further. What I recommended may not fit as well as I thought with the initial information I had. With the new details you shared, we can look at other options that may suit your needs better."

Your Answer to the objection may be clear-cut where you explain certain details or information. As you Answer, use the Whats to WiifTs format discussed in Chapter 8 to connect the details to the What's in it for Them.

At other times you might not have an Answer, there may be several options that could work, or a resolution is not available. These are the situations when your Answer is a collaborative discussion with Them to identify alternatives or change the scope of the solution.

That's how Stop, Drop, and Roll, illustrated in Figure 9–2, keeps the conversation collaborative. It's a strategy we can employ at any point in the conversation when an objection or question is stated, not just during the *Facilitate* step.

Figure 9–2 Stop, Drop, Roll™

Stop	**Drop**	**Roll**
Pause & Listen	Assumptions, Agendas & Emotions	with Acknowledge, Ask & Answer

Your approach to any objection is going to either move you through the objection collaboratively or create a barrier that you will need to climb over at some point. Using Stop, Drop, and Roll with Acknowledge, Ask, and Answer removes all barriers and advances you through the rest of the WIIFT conversation.

✓ TIMELY TIP

To *Facilitate* through an objection *within a group*, you also want to Stop, Drop, and Roll. Stop, then Drop the agenda, emotions, and assumptions. Roll with an Acknowledgment of the objection, and then Ask your clarifying question, first to the person stating the objection and then to the rest of the group if necessary. Group members may resolve the objection among themselves. If not, continue to Ask and Answer as appropriate. Then Roll forward to the rest of the conversation.

PREPARE TO WORK THROUGH OBJECTIONS

Preparing for possible objections increases your probability of working through them effectively during the conversation. The Quick Prep Tool, Figure 12–1 in Chapter 12, guides you through the entire conversation, including preparation for possible objections that might surface in a specific conversation.

To prepare for objections:

1. *Identify probable objections or questions that might be raised* in this specific conversation.

2. *Write open-ended clarifying questions* you can ask if a concern or question is raised.

3. *Identify additional Investigate questions* you might ask during the Investigation to discover and discuss information before it becomes an objection or obstacle in the Facilitate step.

4. *Prepare proof or validation materials* to be incorporated into your conversation to eliminate the objection before it surfaces or when working through a stated objection.

Preparation (the habit you will grow to love when you consistently do it) helps you to remain collaborative at the right moment in the conversation and sales process.

Preparing for possible objections worked for an international seller who had been moving through WIIFT with a buyer for months. As he prepared for the *Facilitate* step and his demo on the prototype, he identified the possible objections the buyer might have and how he would respond.

During the demo, the buyer raised one of the expected objections and the seller was able to calmly Stop, Drop, and Roll. He paused, acknowledged that he understood what the buyer said, asked for clarity on specific points, and then answered with a request for help in identifying ideas on how to address the objection.

The buyer sent the seller a note the following day with several ideas that he and his team had brainstormed. The buyer's solution to his own objection resolved it and the sale moved forward.

In addition to preparing for specific conversations, you can prepare for the most common objections or questions raised in your sales conversations. Each time you hear an objection, make note of it. Then:

•   Research information such as proof points, examples of alternatives, pricing options, and policies that may help you work through the objection in different situations and with different buyers.

- Talk with others in your company or industry who may hear the same objections. Ask them how they work through it. Ask them for information on the types of proof they use and resolutions they have found work well. This information may save you time and effort.

For example, if the objection is cost, research how those costs were determined—it's rarely an arbitrary number someone in Finance decided to stick on the product. Then use case studies, past experiences from other buyers, and research within the industry to identify the value the solution has brought to others. When you hear the cost objection, you will be able to Stop, Drop, and Roll by asking the right clarifying questions and providing supporting data to work through the objection or question on cost.

Building your knowledge for common objections allows you to be a better problem resolver the next time you hear that specific objection.

TAP INTO EMOTIONS THAT AFFECT WORKING THROUGH OBJECTIONS

There are many emotions involved during the entire sales process—excitement, anticipation, fear, frustration, confidence, disappointment, and irritation are a few. These emotions can escalate when an objection is voiced. In fact, these emotions may be a hindrance to working through objections. *How* we work with the buyer's emotions influences how likely we are to work through the objections with Them.

Working with the logical *and* emotional influences of the buyer is important throughout the sales process—and especially when the buyer has objections. Stop, Drop, and Roll guides you through addressing both of these factors. Yet sometimes working with emotions is an obstacle in itself. You may have been taught that the buyer should be "mirrored" or matched emotion for emotion throughout the sales process. Do you really want to match anger with anger, frustration with more frustration, or irritation with irritability?

Probably not. Matching those emotions would hurt your ability to work through the objection. What often works is *adjusting your level of intensity*.

Communicate with Intensity

Many communication "misses" and escalated objections are caused by a mismatch of *intensity*, one aspect of emotions. The following situation from a retail sale is a good example:

> BUYER (with a medium tone and loudness): "You just gave me the wrong product after a long wait. I'd like a refund."

> SELLER (very calmly): "Yes, there was an error in fulfillment. What would you like us to do?"

> BUYER (louder and more anxiously): "I would like you to take back this product and give me a refund like I asked."

> SELLER (very calmly with a lower voice): "Well, we can do that and the refund will take thirty days to process through your account."

> BUYER (incredulous and loud): "I don't think *you* get this. I have already paid and waited thirty minutes and now you gave me the wrong item. I want an immediate refund."

> SELLER (extremely calm): "I'm sorry to hear that. Our policy is to issue a credit in thirty days."

> BUYER (irritated and increasingly frustrated): "Well that doesn't make sense!"

Why was the buyer getting more frustrated? The seller was saying some of the right things—in a very calm and low-key way. This calmness caused the buyer to escalate her emotional reaction and intensity because she didn't think the seller was "getting it." She became more emotional to try to communicate the degree of her frustration.

The seller kept missing my signals of irritation and despair (yes, I was the irritated buyer). What I needed to know was that he understood that the gift I was expecting to give my husband for his birthday wasn't available and I didn't know what to do. I needed empathy and understanding, not a refund thirty days later.

The disconnection in intensity led to misunderstanding, less engagement, and loss of business (I still won't go to that store, five years later). He wasn't really *hearing* me. Yes, he listened to my words, but he wasn't getting the intensity and emotions that told the real story and the importance of the purchase.

Had the seller been more animated and emphasized his concern with an increase in tone and energy, we might have headed in a more mutually agreeable direction. I would have felt that he cared and that I mattered.

What does this information on intensity mean for all of us? When something goes wrong or there is an objection, when we try to understand and connect with the person, we increase their level of satisfaction and loyalty, even if we can't resolve the problem.

Showing some intensity isn't only important when working with complaints. It's also about excitement! If you are presenting a solution and notice the energy or level of intensity changing in your buyer, pay attention and adjust your intensity. The adjustment might need to be up or down; getting to the right level is what matters.

Sometimes I see sellers get more intense and animated when the buyer begins to back off or seems uninterested, thinking that intensity will generate a higher level of interest. This mismatch of intensity usually backfires, accelerates distrust, and causes the buyer to dismiss the discussion as superficial.

We don't need to match the same level of intensity. We need to increase our intensity enough to show that we "get it." This means becoming more animated, making more direct eye contact, and raising the pitch in our voice a bit.

Long story short: We need to *adjust our intensity level*, not get emotional with Them.

SKIP THE "BUTS" THAT HINDER COLLABORATION

A single word can ignite a defensive emotional reaction. If your Acknowledgment statement is followed by "but" or "however," that one word can negate your acknowledgment and send the message, "I hear you and now I'm going to tell you why you are wrong." It lowers trust and collaboration and creates a fight-or-flight response from the buyer.

"But" or "however" in a sentence contradicts the first part of your Acknowledgment. Often the word "but" is simply inserted as a connector between two statements, not as a contradictor. The problem is that your buyers don't have time to figure out which part of the statement is the real message, so most focus on the last part of what you say. We don't want to shut down our collaborative selling approach with just one word. For instance:

- "I know you want a lower price, *but* the economy is affecting everything and my hands are tied."

- "I appreciate you asking that question, *but* I don't know the answer."

- "I'm sorry you don't like the answer, *but* that's all I can do."

The big question then is . . . how do we Acknowledge we hear Them and segue into a response or question? There are two simple approaches:

1. End your Acknowledgment with a pause (or use a period in writing). Then, after the pause, start the second sentence with a segue into your clarifying question.

2. Use the word "and" to connect the Acknowledgment and the statement that follows.

By using these two approaches to skipping the "buts," here's how the above examples would be restated:

- "I know you want a lower price. *(pause)* The economy has made budgeting so much more challenging. Let's explore your options for staying within your budget."

- "I appreciate you asking the question *and* there may be some ways for us to address what you ask. Let's look at how."

- "I'm sorry you do not like the answer *and* I have done what I can. An option for you is to_____."

The use of "but" as a connector is a bad habit, one that might jeopardize your success in working through the concern or objection. "Skipping the buts" takes effort and is well worth that effort. The payoff is a clear message from you and a conversation that continues.

Although we sellers should avoid the use of "but," we need to listen up when the buyer uses it, because they are using "but" to begin an objection or to ask a question. When you hear a "but," use Stop, Drop, and Roll to work through the objection or question that follows it.

STRATEGIES TO WORK THROUGH OBJECTIONS WITH THE TRIBAL TYPES

Ever notice how much variation there is in the reaction from different buyers when objections or questions surface? Tribal Type customs are an even greater factor when the buyer feels they are under pressure. Their need for certain types of information, their preferences for how they work with others, and their fears determine how they approach an objection. The good news is that you can adjust your Stop, Drop, and Roll delivery for each Type.

Achievers are decisive and want to get it done. They may think that concerns or questions are time-wasters. You may find that they express concerns or objections before hearing all the information, get frustrated when there isn't an immediate answer, don't raise concerns at times because they don't want to slow down the progress, or want to push to an answer without exploring options.

To work through objections with Achievers:

- Let them know that concerns will be addressed quickly.

- Ask for their ideas on possible solutions to the concern or objection.

- Clarify what the real concern is and discuss the impact of results and time frame.

Commanders will want the solution to be "right." They will analyze the solution from all angles, ask a lot of "why" questions, willingly express their objection or question when asked, may say "let me think about this first," and are firm in their opinion.

To work through objections with Commanders:

- Ask clarifying questions with a factual and logical approach.

- Ask for opinions and suggestions for resolutions to the concern or objection.

- Let the solution be their idea.

- Be factual and logical in your approach.

Reflectors do not want to rush or confront. They may not state their objections or questions unless they are asked. You may find that they avoid potential conflict, agree easily even if it is to their disadvantage, prefer time to consider options, and are not comfortable being put on the spot.

To work through objections with Reflectors:

- Express your Acknowledgment of the objection or question with feeling and empathy.

- Reassure them (through body language and words) that their concerns are valid and will be addressed.

- Discuss fears and potential risks.

Expressers do not like potential conflict or confrontation. They do not want to hurt your feelings—even though they may have objections. They may agree with you and go along with a commitment . . . for now. Then you may find that they stall when it comes to taking action, don't return phone calls or messages, become less open with information, or involve others later rather than sooner.

To work through objections with Expressers:

- Ask for questions or concerns assertively.

- Assure them you want to work through any potential concerns *with* Them and that everyone can succeed and win.

- Demonstrate (through body language and words) the desire to collaborate.

- Use "feeling" words and "Who" questions like: "What types of questions do you feel others might have about this?" or "Who else should be involved in giving feedback on what we've recommended?"

Subtle changes in how you Acknowledge, Ask, and Answer with each Tribal Type make a huge difference in their willingness to work with you.

TRAPS TO AVOID WHEN FACED
WITH OBJECTIONS AND CONCERNS

Stop, Drop, and Roll is helpful for working through objections and questions, yet there are traps and blind spots that will diminish your effectiveness if you aren't aware of them. Using Stop, Drop, and Roll will keep you from falling into the traps of assumptions, past experience bias, and responding too quickly.

Assumptions You may have heard the objection or question hundreds, if not thousands, of times. For Them, it's their first time and they need you to work them through it, without shortcutting the process. Avoid making assumptions about what they are saying or what the real objection is. Assumptions stop us from listening and clarifying the objection or question. Our assumption in "where this is going" may be wrong. Take the time to listen and clarify the objection or question.

Past Experience Biases Your relationship and experiences with an existing buyer creates its own set of assumptions that impact your emotional reaction to their objections. You may think "here we go again" or "she always does this." Though knowing their pattern can help you in preparing for potential objections, once you are actually having the conversation, remain open to objectively finding out more about the what and why of this particular objection or question.

Responding Too Quickly In the effort to resolve the situation quickly, we may prematurely make commitments to a deal. This leads to unnecessary discounts and unrealistic delivery expectations. Stop when they state their objection, pause (take a breath if you need to), and then Acknowledge.

TURN OBJECTIONS INTO OPPORTUNITIES

Facilitating through an objection successfully begins in your mind. How you *think* about objections factors heavily into your reaction to objections. The words "objections" and "negotiation" often have negative connotations.

Some of the concepts you might associate with these words are "manipulation," "confrontation," or "winners and losers," for example. These thoughts do not lead to the mindset needed for collaborative problem resolution.

Instead of these negative thoughts, think of objections as an *opportunity* to:

- *Collaborate* with your buyer as a problem resolver.

- *Strengthen your connection* with the buyer as you focus on Their ideas, concerns, and feelings.

- *Educate* yourself and the buyer. Perhaps we need to learn something from them because we didn't ask or they didn't share specific details earlier. Or the buyer needs to learn something or have more information about the solution, proof, or details that were not explained to the level they needed.

- *Show expertise.* Our ability to work through objections collaboratively and by sharing examples, ideas, and suggestions shows our flexibility, knowledge, and experience.

Converting objections into opportunities for collaborative problem resolution takes skill and discipline. We may need to train ourselves to respond differently than we naturally would. It takes some effort and preparation to respond to and work through objections effectively.

We increase our probability of success when we work through objections with a collaborative, opportunity-focused mindset.

QUICK TIPS TO WORK EFFECTIVELY THROUGH OBJECTIONS

- Stop, Drop, and Roll when you hear an objection, concern, or question.

- Acknowledge the buyer's objection, ask for clarification, and then Answer appropriately.

- Show (by your level of intensity) that you understand their objection, are listening, and that you really hear Them.

- Skip the "buts" and "howevers" after you Acknowledge their objection.

- Adjust the delivery of Stop, Drop, and Roll to the customs of the buyer's Tribal Type.

- Develop the mindset that you add more value to the buyer's experience when you view the objection as an opportunity to be an effective problem *resolver.*

CHAPTER 10

Then Consolidate: Close Every Conversation with Purpose

"Decisions determine destiny."
—Frederick Speakman, **author**

After all the hard work in collaborating with your buyer through the WIIFT steps, it would be a shame to not wrap up the conversation as purposefully as you began it. Your last step in WIIFT, *Then Consolidate*, guides you to a productive conversation closure—and a sale.

Your conversations count more to buyers when you use their time productively. A productive conversation ends with Them making a decision or commitment to *do* something. Talking about their POWNs only helps them if they make a decision—the buying decision or a decision advancing the sale—that leads to a solution for their POWNs. The lack of a decision prolongs the sales cycle and frustrates the buyer, you, and your sales manager.

I've observed too many sellers who work hard to build the relationship, identify the POWNs, demonstrate their solutions' value, and then wait . . ., follow up with the buyer, wait . . ., follow up with the buyer again, and then wait some more. What they don't do is *ask* for a decision or commitment to advance or make the sale.

When I ask sellers, "What keeps you from closing more sales?" I often hear, "The buyers don't make timely decisions."

Yet, when I ask buyers why they didn't buy a solution, their response is often, "They never asked me!"

Then Consolidate is your guide to advancing or making the sale by asking for and securing the decision or commitment. It also assists you in setting the right expectations by identifying next steps, strengthening the relationship, and closing the conversation.

Why "consolidate" instead of "close"? Closing sales is typically an outcome—securing the buy decision. But *Then Consolidate* is more; it's the step that unites all the previous steps to easily advance or make the sale.

Consolidating is how you both close the sale today and open future sales opportunities with that buyer. *Consolidating* opens the door as you close the sale.

KNOW WHAT YOU ARE CLOSING

Not every sales conversation ends with a buy decision; there may be multiple conversations and a series of decisions before the final decision is made. That's why your preparation, the focus of the *Wait* step introduced in Chapter 5, *begins* with identifying the desired outcome for the conversation. Clarifying your desired outcome ensures you have the right conversation to result in the successful outcome you seek.

Typical desired sales conversation outcomes include:

- *Getting the buy decision* (securing the order).

- *Fact-finding* for specific information about POWNs (qualifying the buyer for budget and decision-making authority).

- *Collaborating* through a discussion of how your solution addresses their POWNs (facilitating the presentation or recommendation of your solution and the plan for its implementation).

- *Achieving an introduction* to someone else (earning the opportunity for the influencer to introduce you to the implementer, the spouse, the final decision maker, or other group or committee members involved in the final decision).

I've always been amazed at how little preparation is put into ending a sales conversation and how many sales are stalled or lost because of it. Knowing what you want or need to close identifies your goal for the conversation. It's the start to successfully completing WIIFT and closing the sale.

FIVE ACTIONS THAT CONSOLIDATE YOUR WIN³ CONVERSATIONS

Consolidating is important because without a final purchase decision a Win³ may not be achieved: the buyer never receives the value of your solution, you never get in the champion's circle or president's club, and your company loses a potential customer and sale. The five Actions of *Then Consolidate* guarantee a productive closure to each conversation:

1. Complete a decision readiness check.

2. Confirm the value your solution will provide.

3. Ask for a decision or commitment to action.

4. Identify the next steps with specifics.

5. Close the conversation.

ACTION 1: COMPLETE A DECISION READINESS CHECK

Consolidating begins with identifying whether your buyer is ready to make a decision or commitment. Rather than a "trial close," as it's sometimes called, I think of it as a readiness check because that is what we need to do— determine if they are ready to move forward in making a decision or if something is holding them back. The decision readiness check (the check-in) also keeps you from overselling and possibly losing the sale.

In WIIFT, we don't close until we know the buyer is ready. The check-in is your opportunity to continue to involve them as you test the waters before asking for a decision, ensuring you have accomplished what you both needed. Often the readiness check guides the buyer to make the decision then and there. If they are not ready, you may need to move back to a previous step in the WIIFT system.

How do you check in to determine when someone is ready to make a decision? By paying attention to the buyer:

1. Look for body language signals.

2. Listen for readiness words and sounds.

3. Ask readiness questions and listen for the responses.

Look for Body Language Signals

Paying attention to the buyer's communication signals is important throughout the entire conversation, and perhaps even more so at the end. If you meet with your buyers face to face, observing the clues they send with their body gives you some insight into their state of readiness.

Positive body language signals include more relaxed movements, making eye contact with you, leaning toward you, and smiling. Buyers also send clues such as collecting their papers, looking at their phone or clock, making impatient body movements, making eye contact between buyers, standing up, or closing their laptop to indicate they want the conversation to end.

Our dilemma in reading body language is that we don't know if they want to end the conversation because they have what they need and are ready to move forward in the sale, because they have made a "no" decision, or because they have just run out of time. We need to build on our visual check-in with verbal clues.

TIMELY TIP

Body language clues can be misread. A head nodding "yes" doesn't mean the buyer is agreeing with you: it means they are agreeing with what they are thinking. In some cultures, a head nodding is simply a way of sending the "I hear you" signal and being respectful.

Listen for Readiness Words and Sounds

If you are one of the millions of sellers who never sees your buyer, visual messages are nonexistent. That's why words and other sounds are valuable clues for identifying readiness. And if you are fortunate to be in the same room with your buyer, matching your visual observations with words and sounds provides a more accurate check-in.

Buyers send clues about their readiness with the words they use. They may talk as if they are already using your solution or *owning* it. Phrases and questions that indicate they are in an ownership mindset are:

- "When we use this . . ."

- "It looks like we could start . . ."

- "Our purchase order process is a bit cumbersome, but we can make it work."

- "How do your payment terms work?"

- "This is more complete, effective, or less expensive than what we use/do now."

What buyers say is a clue to their readiness to move forward. *How* they communicate at this point of the conversation is also important:

- *Pauses* and *hesitations* in their speech may indicate unstated concerns or questions.

- An *increase in their pace of speech* could signal that they are ready to move forward and would like you to move things along. Or it could mean that they want to end the conversation because they have made a "no" decision.

- The *confidence in their voice* is a gauge of their certainty in making a decision.

- *Background noises*, such as shuffling papers or keyboard clicking, are clues that may indicate they are distracted and no longer paying attention and that they need the conversation to end.

These are signals that help determine readiness. Yet, we still don't know if the words and sounds mean they are *really* ready unless we *ask* Them.

Ask Readiness Questions and Listen to the Responses

By matching the clues of body language and the buyer's words and sounds with a check-in (readiness) question, you confirm what you are observing. Responses to readiness questions clearly identify where buyers are in their thoughts—and in the decision process as well. Readiness questions also check for any final objections or concerns.

Here are some thought-starters for readiness questions:

- "Have we covered all the information you need to make a decision/move forward?"

- "How does what we've discussed sound to you?"

- "What concerns do you have about this solution or about me/my company?"

- "What barriers do you see in implementing this?"

- "What else do you need to know?"

- "Are there any open items we need to cover?"

- "How does this solution align with your goals for _____?"

- "How do you feel/what do you think about the solution we've presented?"

- "How does our proposal line up with your expectations?"

- "What are your next actions in making a decision?"

- "Have we provided all the details you need to know for us to move forward?"

Notice there are both closed- and open-ended questions listed. The open-ended readiness questions provide the buyer with the opportunity to tell you more about the *why* of their level of readiness.

Closed-ended readiness questions are also helpful because we need to start hearing "yes" or "no"—and so does the buyer. When buyers hear themselves say "yes," they often talk themselves into the decision and ask you for the next step in buying at this point. It's powerful persuasion.

If you hear "yes" and positive feedback, then move to the next Action in *Then Consolidate*.

If you hear "no," move back a step or two in WIIFT. You may need to learn more in *Investigate* or refocus the buyer on the value and work through additional objections in *Facilitate*. That's okay. Revisiting previous WIIFT steps helps you move forward when the time is right.

Readiness questions are aimed at keeping the conversation collaborative, building *your* confidence in asking for the decision, and ensuring you aren't overselling. (It took a few tough situations for me to realize that many buyers don't want to prolong this part of the process, they want to "get it done!")

ACTION 2: CONFIRM THE VALUE
YOUR SOLUTION WILL PROVIDE

Positive responses from the decision readiness check move you into the decision arena. Segue into the decision question by confirming the value of your solution is an effective segue into the decision question. This provides one last reminder of why they should make a decision now.

Confirm by recapping what you've discussed and reinforcing the value or the WiifT:

- "Chris, as we reviewed, our three-step fertilizer program will yield you between 10 and 15 percent more crop this growing season."

- "Your investment in advertising to a targeted audience in the magazine will expose your company to 150,000 potential customers a month."

Confirming the value reminds buyers of what they will really receive— a solution that addresses their POWNs. The perceived value of your solution increases when you confirm the WiifTs—and so does the likelihood that they will buy.

In the two examples above, the real value that they receive is:

- Increased crop yields, not just fertilizer.

- Potential new customers, not just an ad in a magazine.

Many concerns, fears, and stalls are removed as you remind buyers one final time "What's in it for Them." This is an effective setup to asking for the decision or commitment.

ACTION 3: ASK FOR A DECISION OR COMMITMENT TO ACTION

Asking for a decision or action naturally follows the confirmation of value: It keeps you from sounding random or disjointed. "Do you want this?" or "Ready to sign the papers?" without a segue can make the buyer feel defensive. Instead, confirm the value of your solution and then ask for the decision:

- "Chris, as we reviewed, our three-step fertilizer program will yield you between 10 and 15 percent more crop this growing season. Are you ready to place the order?"

- "Your investment in advertising to a targeted audience in the magazine will expose your company to 150,000 potential customers a month. Should we design your campaign to begin with next month's issue?"

The easiest and most efficient way to close more sales or advance your sale is to complete the earlier steps of WIIFT and then ask the buyer to make a decision or commitment.

A decision is what is needed. A "no" response is better than no answer because then you can move on to more probable opportunities. If you get a "yes," you've just closed another sale.

To confidently and successfully ask for a decision:

- *Be specific.* Clearly ask for a specific decision or action, such as "Are you ready to move forward?" or "Can we initiate the paperwork today?"

- *Be assertive in asking for the decision.* Asking a complex question such as, "Are you ready to make the next step or *do you need more information?*" complicates the situation and indicates insecurity.

- *Pause after asking the decision question and wait for Them to respond.* Do not minimize the importance of making a decision or try to rush them.

- *Use a confident tone.* The responses to your readiness questions should have removed your fear of a negative response. Keep your voice steady.

- *Make eye contact* when you ask.

- *Adapt your question* to their Tribal Type.

Securing this decision verbally is important. If the buyer doesn't specifically answer, then you are moving forward on assumptions—and you know what happens when we assume, don't you? We can be wrong and set ourselves up for disaster.

This lesson was reinforced as I sat behind the exit row on an airplane. Before the plane departed, the flight attendant approached the passengers in the exit rows to explain their role in case of an emergency. She then asked them if they were willing to help others in an emergency. All four passengers nodded their head in agreement.

Then the attendant said, "I need you to verbally tell me 'yes' or 'no.'" And they each said, "Yes."

As I watched this situation, I thought, "That's what's often missing in closing sales. We pay attention to body language and make assumptions. But if we don't have a verbal commitment or agreement, we might be setting ourselves up for a disaster later."

Many buyers need us to ask them to make that verbal commitment to action or a decision. Whether the decision is a buy decision, a commitment to a next meeting, an introduction to someone else, or permission to send additional information, we need Them to say "yes."

Help the Tribal Types Make Decisions

Getting that decision can be rewarding—and frustrating! There are many factors that affect decision making:

- Emotions

- Their trust level with you

- The belief that what you offer will help with their POWNs

- Budget

- Internal politics

Don't ignore emotions' impact on decision making. Use what you learned about their emotional hot buttons and risks or rewards in the *Investigate* step to address and influence the emotions and logic components. My observation is that decisions are not always made logically. Often they are made with emotion and then supported with logic. The emotions can be positive or negative; some people move forward with excitement or joy while others may be driven more by fear or other negative emotions.

You impact the buyer's decision making as well. Some buyers won't make a decision without your proactive approach in asking for the commitment. Others don't want you to complicate the process and want you to get out of their way. Tribal Type customs provide insight into how different people approach and reach decisions. This insight allows you to vary your approach in asking for the decision.

Achievers *Achievers* make quick and impulsive decisions. They hear something that resonates with them and they are ready to "Just do it," as Nike says. While this is beneficial in securing a quick buying decision, there are some pitfalls. For example, wrong expectations can be set or others in their buying company/family may not buy in and may challenge the decision.

Achievers fear being taken advantage of or delaying a decision and failing to achieve something on time.

To aid Achievers at decision time:

- Provide only the most important information to them.

- Don't overcomplicate the decision-making process.

- Make it easy for them by taking care of the details or paperwork, if possible.

- It might be necessary to hold up the caution sign; let them know that slowing down now to address other information may prove beneficial later.

- Ask, "What would you like to do next?"

Commanders *Commanders* like to make the right decision. Their need to be right might mean that decision making is a long process that includes lots of facts, evidence, analysis, and more analysis. Commanders like options and the ability to make a comparison. They also like the final decision to be their idea, so the opinions of others carry little weight. Their need to be right can also be a blind spot that blocks out relevant information—even if the information supports what they want to do.

Commanders fear being wrong. They need to make a sound and correct decision, but their decisions aren't always as logical as they believe.

To aid Commanders at decision time:

• Provide information they need, preferably in printed copy.

• Take a logical and organized approach to the process that leads to the decision.

• Use quantifiable information whenever possible for describing the value provided by your solution and the return on their investment.

• Present options for them to select from.

• Ask "What other information would be helpful as you weigh your options?"

Reflectors *Reflectors* need time to make a decision. Because they don't like risk and want to be careful, they need information, detail, and others' input to comfortably make the decision. The bigger the decision, the more information, detail, and input they will need. The "buy now or you lose out" approach does not work well with them, and they will decide *not* to do something if pushed. The delay in making a final decision can be costly, and assisting a Reflector in making a decision is valuable.

Reflectors fear change and instability, which can make every decision feel like a risky one. They worry that something will go wrong after they decide and then they will be stuck.

To aid Reflectors at decision time:

• Clarify the process of what happens after a decision is made.

• Set expectations and be clear on what decision you are seeking.

- Provide the warranty and guarantee details to minimize the perceived risks.

- Be patient and assertive. Though they need time to make the decision, they also appreciate a timeline that forces them to actually decide.

- Ask, "How can I support you as you finalize your decision?" Stay in touch more often than with the other Types.

Expressers *Expressers* make a lot of decisions, and they may reverse many of them as well. They will make a decision "in the moment" that satisfies them and the people with them at that time. If contrary opinions or ideas surface soon after, they can be easily swayed to change their decision. The opinions of the other people involved matter to them. You, the people on your team, and the people affected by the decision are important drivers in a decision.

Be careful. Expressers may tell you how much they like your offering, how great you are, and how much they like this or that. *This isn't necessarily a buying signal.* They don't want to hurt your feelings. Also, Expressers' decisions are often highly emotional and they can be "oversold." Further, Expressers fear making an unpopular decision that will affect how others feel about them.

To aid Expressers at decision time:

- Stay in touch with them to keep you and your solution at the top of their minds. Plan for time to be social in your contacts rather than "all business."

- Offer your opinion. They may even ask "What would you do?" or "Do you use this?"

- Find out who else needs to be involved and involve them as early on as possible in the sales process.

- Since Expressers are visual, they like to see the solution when possible— use tangible sales aids or paint the picture with a story that they can put themselves into. Highlight and condense the most important items for them. Too much detail or lengthy reports or handouts will most likely not be read. Then equip them with more details to "sell it up" internally if they need to.

- Ask, "What will others think about doing this?" Positive opinions from others will spur them on; negative ones are better out in the open so you can address them (collaboratively, of course).

Recognizing the customs of each Tribal Type helps you to address the logical and emotional factors. Adjust how you work with the buyer through all the WIIFT steps and then ask for the decision. This proactive request moves stalled sales, increases your closing success, and strengthens the value you bring to the sales process.

ACTION 4: IDENTIFY THE
NEXT STEPS WITH SPECIFICS

Depending on what you sell, a decision may just be the beginning of your real work.

Once you have a decision, your job is not over, there is still more to do to keep the process moving forward: You need to clearly identify *who* is doing *what* by when.

Identify the next steps that you and the buyer will take after the conversation to ensure the order is fulfilled as promised. These steps could be creating a purchase order or the buyer making a down payment. Clarify the specifics of the implementation and detail future communication processes to ensure the sale moves forward. This allows you to set the right expectations after a purchase decision has been made and eliminates redundancy and lack of action. It speeds up the purchase process.

Here are several examples of the types of next steps you may need to clarify:

- If your buyer commits to a follow-up meeting with you and their manager, identify the date of the meeting, its objectives, and any information needed beforehand. This ensures that the next meeting will be successful.

- For corporate sales, when the decision is made to use your services, an internal purchasing process may begin. Help the buyer prepare the necessary specific details, specifications, and samples to move it forward internally.

- In consumer sales, identify how they can register for the warranty, make the payment, learn how to use the product, and also where they can get support if needed.

Identifying the next steps keeps your sale moving along.

ACTION 5: CLOSE THE CONVERSATION

Then Consolidate ends with a close . . . every time! The close is the last thing you say before hanging up the phone, leaving their office, or walking away, and this closure does count.

To close the conversation and minimize potential buyer's remorse, let them know they have made a sound or good decision and again restate the value—how their POWNs will be resolved.

Personalize your final statements with specific and relevant comments such as:

- "Thanks for allowing us to _____."
- "I appreciate the time you have given us to _____."
- "I appreciate your arranging a meeting next week with _____."
- "Please do not hesitate to contact me if you have any questions."

You will keep future opportunities open with an invitation and/or question such as:

- "How else might we help you?"
- "What else would you like to discuss?"
- "Please know that you can contact me via email or phone whenever you need."
- "When should I follow up to see if all is going as planned?"
- "What's the best way to stay in contact with you?"

End your conversation as positively as it started with: "Congratulations," "Thank you," or "I appreciate _____." Include a specific and personal reason why you are congratulating or thanking them. According to 2010 research from the *Journal of Marketing*, flattery works!

✓ TIMELY TIP

The power of a sincere "Congratulations!" is underestimated. Congratulating your buyer on a decision or commitment is a powerful way to strengthen their confidence that they've made the best decision in moving forward. To make it more powerful, send a note of congratulations after the conversation.

* * *

Then Consolidate is the final step to successfully bring your sales conversation to closure. Keep in mind that one run-through of WIIFT often is not enough:

- Once your decision is secured, you might start the whole process over again with a new POWN, buying team, or procurement.

- You may uncover a new POWN at the end of your conversation and need to circle back to *Investigate, Facilitate,* and *Then Consolidate* again.

WIIFT is a conversation framework and a strategic road map to track your major stopping points within multiple sales cycles. Follow the five steps of WIIFT in every buyer conversation to advance or make your sale.

QUICK TIPS FOR CONSOLIDATING YOUR CONVERSATIONS

- Pay attention to the emotional and logical factors that impact decision making. Different fears come into play, and your ability to Stop, Drop, and Roll with any final objections or concerns will alleviate those fears.

- Summarize and then assertively *ask* for the decision. Then wait. Forward movement and action is the goal—for you and your buyers.

- Clearly identify next steps and don't leave anything hanging.

- Follow up with a written confirmation of the next actions after the conversation. This is especially appreciated by Commanders and Reflectors and may be necessary to keep the Expressers and Achievers on track.

- Eliminate decision questions that ask for two competing decisions, such as "Are you ready to take the next step or *do you not have enough information*?" or "Should I start the paperwork or *do you need to include someone else*?" Being vague or unclear as to what you are asking for may give them an easy out.

- Close your conversation with a personalized statement or invitation to keep the door open to future opportunities.

PART III

The Factors That Make or Break Your Sales

CHAPTER 11

Will You or Won't You Succeed?
It's Your Choice

*"The outer conditions of a person's life will
always be found to reflect their inner beliefs."*
—JAMES LANE ALLEN, **British writer and pioneer of the self-help movement**

What does it really take to be successful in sales? This question is one of the great debates in the sales community.

Sales managers, business owners, and global sales groups on LinkedIn regularly tackle highly debated issues such as: Is selling an art or a science? Are salespeople born or made? Is knowledge or skill more important in selling success? What is the *one* characteristic all sellers must have?

The list of "musts" and "what it takes" in these debates is so long that it's impossible to select one definitive answer to any of the questions. What is consistent, though, is that the responses to these queries include specific competence and confidence factors. I call these the "Skill and Will" factors for sales success.

"SKILL AND WILL": THE DYNAMIC
DUO OF SALES SUCCESS

"Skill and Will" are the dynamic duo of sales success. They provide an easily remembered phrase to refer to the factors that lead to top performance in sales.

Skill is your competence. It is the knowledge of *what* to do and your effectiveness in being able to put that knowledge into productive and consistent action.

Skills can be learned, observed, and easily evaluated from the outside. It's what most of this book has focused on—skills in collaborative WIIFT conversations adjusted for Tribal Types.

Skill is important, yet equally important is the *Will* to perform.

Will is the confidence and drive to take action. Will is *why* you do what you do—it's internally based and is invisible to the outside world.

In most sales teams, I find that the seller who knows the most is often *not* the seller who sells the most. The most successful sellers are those who have the required knowledge *and* take the necessary actions. They:

- Prospect.

- Prepare for conversations and overall strategy.

- Use a consistent and collaborative conversation approach.

- Build relationships in and outside their company.

- Make contact each day with prospective buyers.

- Ask for decisions.

- Follow up.

- Continue to learn.

The commitment to these actions and the consistency in taking them is impacted more by the Will factor than the Skill factor. The Will factor is the amplifier of sales skills. Take two sellers with the same Skill and I can accurately predict that the one with a stronger Will factor is the better performer.

The Will factor's impact can be observed in sports by looking at Wisconsin's much beloved football team, the Green Bay Packers. In January 2012 they had all the Skill they needed to reach the Super Bowl for a second straight year, but when they walked onto the field of a playoff game, I noticed that their Will seemed lacking. Their energy was low, they were tentative, and they didn't appear to be fired up. Within the first few minutes I said, "They aren't going to win this one." And they didn't. Why was their Will lower that day? I don't know, but I know I could feel it in their actions and energy; they weren't "in the zone" that day.

THE SUCCESS DRIVERS OF
TOP SALES PROFESSIONALS

Being "in the zone" is typically a sports reference, yet it's also relevant to being most productive and successful in work and in life. The *zone* is a state of total focus and effortless performance where your knowledge and skill merge into dominating your challenge or opponent.

Sellers in the zone of sales success are driven to succeed. This success then builds more success and it may seem as if they have a magic touch or are just lucky. But, as Thomas Jefferson said, "I'm a great believer in luck, and I find the harder I work the more I have of it."

Action is necessary for being in the zone and succeeding. For example, most sellers will intellectually agree with the tools, steps, and behaviors outlined in this book. They will agree that the earlier list of activities is necessary. What happens next with that knowledge—action or inaction with the information—is the difference between mediocre and stellar performance later.

The Will factor is complex, consisting of several components that I call the *Success Drivers*. The model is called Success Drivers™ because strengthening these components (the Drivers) propels you forward to actions, results, and success.

In studying the top performers among the thousands of sellers I have worked with, I have noticed four common Drivers that help explain why some sellers do what is necessary to succeed, and others don't. (I say "help explain" because the dynamics of sales success and the uniqueness of each seller makes this topic neither as simple nor as formulaic as presented here.) The Success Drivers model shown in Figure 11–1 illustrates the Drivers—Integrated Beliefs (Self, Value, Role), Goal Transparency, Initiative, and Emotional Intelligence—and their relationship to each other.

Figure 11-1 Success Drivers™

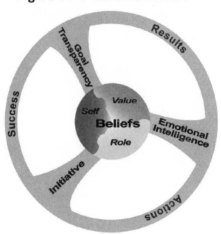

Success starts at the center of the model with Beliefs, a multifaceted internal component that integrates the beliefs you have in *yourself*, in your *role in sales*, and in the *value of your solution*.

They are called Integrated Beliefs because they combine together into one Driver that also has connectivity with the other three Success Drivers: Goal Transparency, Initiative, and Emotional Intelligence.

The four Drivers explain the Will factor that is often the differentiator between top performers and everyone else. Top performers have passion for what they do and what they sell, they are focused on their goals, they are proactive in their efforts, and they do not let their emotions negatively impact their activity level.

Let's look at the Drivers in more detail.

Integrated Beliefs

Confidence is often cited as a key characteristic of a top performer. Does this confidence come from their success or has their success created the confidence? Probably both. Confidence comes from the internal beliefs in *who they are, what they do,* and *why their solution is valuable to others.*

Integrated Beliefs are three beliefs that combine to drive Goal Transparency, Initiative, and Emotional Intelligence. Their integration positively or negatively impacts their effect on your actions.

Belief in Self *Belief in Self* is self-confidence in your abilities and skills to be successful. The value you personally bring to your buyers and customers is reflected in this belief. You are integral to the total value your buyers receive when they buy from you.

To gauge the level of belief in yourself, answer these questions:

- Do you want to be successful?

- Do you see yourself being successful in sales?

- Do you believe that you have the skill or can develop the skill and attitudes to be successful?

- Do you believe that you give value to your customers and prospects in the sales process and beyond?

Confidence in yourself affects your buyer's confidence as well. Busy buyers may identify lack of confidence as weakness, inability, or just a plain waste of their time. If they sense your lack of confidence, they won't feel confident in you or your recommendation.

Belief in Role *Belief in Role* is the belief in your sales role and the value of that role to your company, the buyers, and yourself. As mentioned in the Introduction to this book, reluctant sellers may have a low belief in the value of selling, which impacts their actions and activities needed to succeed.

A strong belief in your role leads to feeling good about what you do.

To gauge the level of belief in your role, listen to how you describe what you do. Do you describe it as a "just" position? "I'm just in sales." Or, "I'm just the person peddling this stuff." Or, "I'm just the liaison." If you don't see that you are integral to the Win[3] through your efforts and role, neither will the buyer—nor will your boss.

Belief in Value *Belief in Value* is the belief in your solution's value in relation to the cost to secure the solution. Your belief that the solution is worth more than its cost matters. For instance, when a new product was launched during the time I was a distributor for a training company, many of us believed it was a premature launch and that the quality of the solution was not up to the standards that our customers expected and valued.

No matter how much the marketing department and the president tried to convince us of the value and threw incentives at us to sell this new course, many of us continued to sell the old one. Because we did not believe in the value of the new version, we could not sell or relate its value to prospects and clients. Sales suffered.

Have you noticed that it is easier for you to sell some of your products or services than others? If you look closely you might find that you have high personal belief in the value of the solutions you are most successful with. That's the effect of the belief in value.

Integrated Beliefs are the core of the Success Drivers model and describe the importance of beliefs in who, what, and why. They are reflected in the passion you have for yourself, your profession, and your solution. Sellers with strong integrated beliefs have confidence and are driven to help as many buyers as possible gain access to their solution.

Because the beliefs integrate, when you strengthen any one of the beliefs, you positively affect the other beliefs. The opposite is also true; if any one of the beliefs is low, the other beliefs suffer as well.

Goal Transparency

Goal Transparency means having written goals that are specific, measurable, and visible to you and others.

Strong Goal Transparency is more than being goal oriented or goal driven. Transparency is demonstrated when your goals are visible to you and others in print, in your actions, and in your words. By sharing your goals and the plans to reach them with your stakeholders, you make the invisible visible and add accountability. A regular review of your goals for relevancy also keeps them timely and valid.

Top performers' goals are transparent. The transparency of their goals gives them stronger accountability to focus on the actions necessary to reach them. They are upfront about what they want to accomplish and if you can help them, great. If you can't, move out of their way! They know where they are headed and will move obstacles that keep them from reaching their goals.

Goal Transparency is key to strengthening your results, commitment, and the other three Drivers. Chapter 13 outlines a goal achievement process that will help you immediately strengthen your Goal Transparency.

Initiative

Initiative is the self-directed, personal, and proactive energy you spend every day. Those with Initiative focus their energy toward proactive and productive activities. They take Initiative and action to complete what is important.

Initiative is an internal drive that some may call motivation. Because it is internal, only *you* can motivate you. Contrary to what many believe, others can't motivate you. Only *you* can find the motivators that rev up your energy. The complexity of this internal driver makes it difficult for an outsider to determine your internal motivators.

Author Daniel Pink addresses this complexity in his book *Drive* (Riverhead Hardcover, 2009). He explains that some are motivated internally to achieve high levels of performance; others are driven to achieve by external rewards. To increase your Initiative, find your personal motivators and then focus on proactive and productive activities to get you where you need or want to go more efficiently.

Top performers take Initiative each day. They face the same priority challenges as everyone else and don't necessarily enjoy some of the mundane parts of selling—like writing follow-up notes, preparation, and plugging information into the company database—any more than others do. What they do, though, is Initiate action on these nondesirables or figure out a way to get them done through other resources because they know these activities will help them succeed. They focus on the most productive activities and get more done to maximize their time and energy.

Emotional Intelligence

Emotional Intelligence (EI) is the awareness of and ability to manage your emotions and their impact on your actions. The importance of EI is supported by the research of the Gearner Group, which found a 73 percent correlation of EI to sales success.

Selling is a tough career. Rejection and success can happen within minutes of each other and the roller coaster of emotions that comes with sales is not always easy to ride. Strong Emotional Intelligence leads to consistency in action and emotionally intelligent sellers don't let their emotions negatively impact their actions.

"Most salespeople know what to do," says Colleen Stanley, author of *Emotional Intelligence for Sales Success* (Amacom, 2013). "However, during stressful selling situations, emotions take over and skills go out the window. Salespeople with good emotion management are able to consistently execute effective skills and behaviors, even with the toughest prospects."

Colleen characterized EI as "knowing what you are feeling, why you are feeling it, and how it affects how you show up."

Important to a strong EI is acknowledging success and progress for your efforts and goals. EI is connected to Goal Transparency and Initiative. As Daniel Pink writes in *Drive*, "On days when workers have the sense they're making headway in their jobs, or when they receive support that helps them overcome obstacles, their emotions are most positive and their drive to succeed is at its peak."

Emotionally Intelligent sellers are aware of their response to outside influences and don't let obstacles, bad days, negative experiences, and rejections stop them. They keep on productively and proactively making decisions and doing what is necessary, even when they don't want to. Their awareness of and ability to manage their emotions in a productive manner is key to their success.

* * *

How do these Success Drivers play out in the real world of sales? Sellers who use their personal Skill and Will to access their unique strengths and preferences succeed when others don't.

Some sellers are more focused on their Skill while others have enough Will to drive them to act and make sales. The long-term high producers use a balance of Skill and Will to consistently achieve their goals. They access their unique strengths and their expertise to add value in each conversation. They know that *they* are a key component in the sales process and that *they* can make every conversation count.

Strength in the four Success Drivers—Integrated Beliefs, Goal Transparency, Initiative, and Emotional Intelligence—drive the right actions that propel you to results and success. If your drive for success is not as high as you would like, you can build each of these Success Drivers with the tips at the end of this chapter.

Skill and Will are the ingredients to success in any endeavor, and both are in your control.

Whether or not you were a "born" sales pro doesn't count as much as whether you are willing to develop yourself into one.

QUICK TIPS TO BUILD YOUR DRIVE TO SUCCEED

- Build belief in yourself: Take time to document your successes for your reference and for performance review time.

- Build belief in your role as a seller: Regularly read sales blogs, forums, and industry publications. Participate in ongoing sales development.

- Build belief in the value of your solution: Make a list of the value your buyers receive from you and your solution.

- Strengthen Goal Transparency: Use the effective goal achievement process outlined in Chapter 13 to write goals and the actions necessary to achieve them, share your goals with stakeholders, and take the actions needed to achieve the goals.

- Increase your Initiative: Stop procrastinating and act! In his book *Eat that Frog!*, author Brian Tracy suggests that you complete the toughest task first each day to release the energy you would spend on avoiding or thinking about the task the rest of the day.

- Boost your Emotional Intelligence: Start a Smile File—a bright yellow file folder to store any notes of thanks, appreciation, job well done, recognition, or successes. On days when your emotional intelligence is low, review the contents to remind yourself of the value you bring.

- While this book isn't specifically about interviewing and coaching, the Success Drivers are a powerful guide for hiring and coaching. I've included specific interview and coaching questions for managers and hiring professionals on the www.conversationsthatsell.com website.

CHAPTER 12

The Tools of the Trade: What's in Your Toolbox?

"If you give people tools, [and they use] their natural ability and their curiosity, they will develop things in ways that will surprise you very much beyond what you might have expected."

—BILL GATES, computer programmer, business magnate, and philanthropist

Though you probably don't carry a hammer, saw, or screwdriver to your sales calls, you do need the right tools to make the conversation count for you and the buyer. In sales, the right tools help you make Win^3 sales more efficiently and effectively.

A tool is anything that helps you get something done. In today's selling world, the term "tools" is synonymous with software and gadgets. While the gadgetry and technology are helpful—and at times even lifesavers— some sellers continue to do very well with just a paper, pen, and Excel spreadsheet.

Whether you are a gadget person or prefer paper and pen, the tools you pull out of your toolbox—your briefcase, hard drive, or mind—need to work for you.

There are many different types of sales tools. The ones I will focus on in this chapter are:

1. *Sales conversation preparation tools* to help you plan and then carry out a productive conversation with your buyer.

2. *Powerful technology-based tools* for territory management, customer relationship tracking, sales process tracking, prospecting, and lead-generating.

3. *Personal assessment tools* for identifying and then capitalizing on the most important sales tool, you!

Though some of you who are committed to the latest applications on tablets or smartphones may find my opinion too simplistic, the specific tools you use don't matter nearly as much as *how* you use the tools.

I have seen far too many companies spend millions of dollars equipping their sales teams with technology that turns out to offer little return on their investment because the sales teams underutilize the new technology (because they won't slow down to learn it, are stuck in old habits, or the tool doesn't deliver). On the opposite end of the spectrum, I've also seen sellers who spend so much time with the latest gadget that it detracts from their selling activities.

What does work is identifying and then committing to the consistent use of the tools in your toolbox.

SALES CONVERSATION PREPARATION TOOLS

Sales conversation preparation tools are used to plan for your conversation with buyers, to guide you during your conversation, and to follow up afterward.

First we'll look at two extremely useful low-tech tools, the Quick Prep Tool™ and the Tribal Types Tool™.

Quick Prep Tool

As English logician and novelist Lewis Carroll said, "If you don't know where you are going, any road will get you there." Fortunately you do know where you are going when you use the two-page Quick Prep Tool, shown in Figures 12–1 and 12–2—you are going into a productive conversation with your buyers.

Figure 12–1 WIIFT Quick Prep™

WIIFT Quick Prep™

Date: _____

Name, Title, Company   Tribal Type©

WAIT   Objective(s) for conversation

Customer POWNs   Need to knows

Value and benefits important to them

INITIATE   3-Step Start notes (greet, why, time/connection questions to open the conversation)

INVESTIGATE   Questions to uncover POWNs - problems, opportunities, wants and needs

1

2

3

4

FACILITATE   Possible recommendation(s)

Possible objections to discuss

THEN CONSOLIDATE   Decision or commitment desired

Follow-up action items
What   Who   When

Figure 12–2 Quick Research™

Quick Research™   Date: _____

Research outlets (company website, social networking groups, company or industry forums or community groups, etc.)

Company information

Review the company's website, brochures, annual reports, and marketing documents, as they provide useful information about:

Mission or value statement

Key stakeholders (names, roles, backgrounds)

Recent company business news (financial results, news releases)

Specific goals (new markets, expansion, returns to stakeholders, personal goals, etc.)

Industry news and trends

For this buyer, what is in alignment with our solution? What potential value do we offer?

Whether you believe preparation is a good idea or that it's just for rookies, low performers, or something you no longer need to do, I can't stress enough that the discipline of preparing for conversations makes *everyone* more productive and efficient.

The Quick Prep Tool's WIIFT Quick Prep™ provides a guide to prepare for the entire WIIFT conversation, while Quick Research™ is an outline of research items for new customers, large opportunities, group selling situations, and stagnant existing buyer conversations.

You can download a copy of the Quick Prep Tool from the www.conversationsthatsell.com website. Or if you want to write really, really small, copy the pages from this book.

Complete the WIIFT Quick Prep page for every face-to-face or telephone conversation you are going to initiate. The steps of WIIFT are outlined to guide you through your preparation for each step. To use this tool effectively, begin with the end in mind by first *identifying the objective* for the conversation. Then write notes in the remaining sections for each step of the WIIFT conversation.

After your conversation, complete the paperwork trail by noting your follow-up action items on the last line. If you have a customer database, input the relevant information directly into your system as soon as possible while it's fresh.

The Quick Research page guides you through productive research items. For opportunities that need more planning, complete this side *before* the WIIFT Quick Prep page. The information you gather from the various research prompts this page provides ensures a relevant conversation for the buyer, saves both of you time, and sets you apart from all the other sellers calling on that buyer.

Following is additional information and tips for each section of Quick Research:

1. *Research outlets.* Identify the sites and resources such as social networking groups, forums, and association and trade sites you will access to conduct your research. Facebook, LinkedIn, and Twitter may offer timely data about the company and for the specific people you will contact.

2. *Company information.* Review the company's website, brochures, annual reports, and marketing documents, as they provide useful information about:

- The *company's mission or value statements.* These statements provide insight into what's important to the company. Are they stewards of the environment, focused on shareholder returns, or employee-centered?

- *Key stakeholders.* Within the buying company, who will care or be impacted by your solution? Who will be the potential influencers when it comes time to make a decision? Look for their bios, roles, and contact information.

- *Recent company business news.* Search for events, a calendar, or public relations links. Look at the annual report, news updates, job openings, or notices to their employees to search for new market focus, expansion or reduction talk, or the returns to stakeholders. Review their financial results/news; quarterly updates and annual reports provide good insight into what happened in the previous year and what they forecast for the next year.

- *Specific goals.* Search the annual report, news updates, and other sources for information for what is important to the company. Look for mentions of new markets, or "new" anything—expansion into new geographies or market segments—and references to their stakeholders. Read the executive team and your buyers' bios for personal goals and what is important to them.

3. *Industry news or trends.* Be a student of the industry you sell in. Search for recent articles or news that may impact the problems, opportunities, wants, or needs of your buyer. Locate forums or social media groups where the thought leaders of your industry share information.

4. *Alignment and value of your solution.* To begin the focus on the buyer and the value you and your solution offer, use the research information to identify preliminary solution matches and the What's in it for Them of the solutions.

For existing buyers, you may also have valuable resources in your company. Review:

- *Your database or CRM system.* What is their history with your company? What and how much have they purchased in the past? Who have they worked with before?

- *Internal associates.* Determine who has worked with this buyer and ask them for tips and history that isn't in the records. Ask them for assistance with making a personal connection.

The potential conversation starters derived from your Quick Research information can open new sales opportunities and increase the sense of urgency for the buyer to implement your solution. For example, the sales team members of a Canadian engineering services company used the research page of the Quick Prep Tool as a guide to search for recent industry news and discovered information about a potential law change that would impact a buyer's risk in product development. By incorporating this information into their presentation with a buyer, they opened a discussion about the new risks that would emerge from the law change. This information increased the buyer's sense of urgency to address a product design issue and the sellers closed the sale in the next visit.

When you make the time to specifically write your meeting notes on Quick Prep Tool pages—moving the plan from your head to the paper—you free your mind during the conversation to listen more effectively, be more collaborative, and provide higher value. It keeps you from missing important information and allows you to be more engaged and flexible during your conversation. If the conversation goes off on a tangent, you can easily refer to your notes to get back on track quickly.

Tribal Types Tool

The Tribal Types model helps you to work with your buyers in the way *they* prefer. Identifying their preferred communication and working customs allows you to adapt your conversations to make every question you ask and every bit of information you share timely and relevant.

The customs for each of the four Tribal Types are easy to learn. Yet our personal biases and quick judgments may complicate our ability to identify the Type. The Tribal Types Tool™ shown in Figure 12–3 provides a quick way to identify the Tribal Type of your prospect (or colleague or sales manager).

Figure 12–3 Tribal Types Tool™

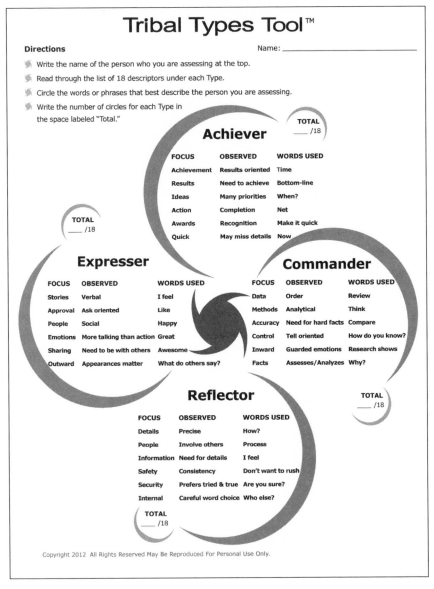

Tribal Types Tool™

Directions   Name: _____

- Write the name of the person who you are assessing at the top.
- Read through the list of 18 descriptors under each Type.
- Circle the words or phrases that best describe the person you are assessing.
- Write the number of circles for each Type in the space labeled "Total."

TOTAL ___ /18

Achiever

FOCUS	OBSERVED	WORDS USED
Achievement	Results oriented	Time
Results	Need to achieve	Bottom-line
Ideas	Many priorities	When?
Action	Completion	Net
Awards	Recognition	Make it quick
Quick	May miss details	Now

TOTAL ___ /18

Expresser

FOCUS	OBSERVED	WORDS USED
Stories	Verbal	I feel
Approval	Ask oriented	Like
People	Social	Happy
Emotions	More talking than action	Great
Sharing	Need to be with others	Awesome
Outward	Appearances matter	What do others say?

Commander

FOCUS	OBSERVED	WORDS USED
Data	Order	Review
Methods	Analytical	Think
Accuracy	Need for hard facts	Compare
Control	Tell oriented	How do you know?
Inward	Guarded emotions	Research shows
Facts	Assesses/Analyzes	Why?

TOTAL ___ /18

Reflector

FOCUS	OBSERVED	WORDS USED
Details	Precise	How?
People	Involve others	Process
Information	Need for details	I feel
Safety	Consistency	Don't want to rush
Security	Prefers tried & true	Are you sure?
Internal	Careful word choice	Who else?

TOTAL ___ /18

To use the Tribal Types Tool, follow these directions:

- Write the name of the person who you are assessing at the top.

- Read through the list of 18 descriptors under each Type.

- Circle the words or phrases that best describe the person you are assessing.

- Write the total number of circles for each Type in the space labeled "Total."

The Tribal Type with the highest score is considered the dominant Type. If two Tribal Types have equal scores it means that both sets of customs are important to that person.

People are a mix; it is highly unusual to find one person with all 18 descriptors in one Tribal Type. Yet it is very likely to see that some customs from all four of the Tribal Types apply to that person.

There are many strategies for selling and working with each of the Tribal Types discussed in detail in Chapter 4. As you prepare for your conversations, incorporate the specific customs into the level of detail you will discuss and divulge, the types of materials you have available, the time allotted for the conversation, and the level of personal relationship you want or need to build.

Complete a Tribal Types Tool before your conversation to prepare the most relevant connection and investigative questions. You can also prepare information and proof according to their customs—using charts, stories, graphics, back-up detail, and reference names that they need.

If you don't have any clues to work from prior to your first conversation, ask people who have worked with or connected with the buyer for ideas on how to best work with them. Then be sure to complete the Tribal Types Tool *following* your conversation as preparation for your follow-up and future conversations.

Download a printable PDF of the Tribal Types Tool from the www. conversationsthatsell.com website.

POWERFUL TECHNOLOGY-BASED TOOLS

The tools to engage and make your conversations more relevant to your buyers are constantly evolving. No longer do you need to have a trunk full of brochures or expensive and time-draining mailings. Today's tech tools allow you to plan and deliver just what is needed for your buyers.

The tools for managing your entire sales process have streamlined paperwork and reporting. There are dozens of helpful lead-generation, customer management, reporting, and territory management tools now available.

One of the early adopters of technology to equip and monitor his sales team is Rick Wohlner of Precision Laboratories. Rick is in the agricultural chemical business—perhaps not what might come to mind when you think of quickly adopting technology. Yet Rick equipped his team with iPads and iPhones to maximize their impact with customers. Most of Precision's sales conversations are with small groups, which makes the iPad an ideal tool for their salespeople to demo and share their literature, slide deck, and playbook. Through video, the sellers also bring the corporate experts into each conversation if needed.

Because technology-based sales tools are constantly evolving, whatever I write about today will be old news by the time the book is published. What won't get old is a fabulous website resource, SmartSellingTools.com (www.smartsellingtools.com), where Nancy Nardin, considered the leading expert on sales productivity tools, provides details of marketing and sales software tools. You will also find up-to-date information and helpful links to other sales tool resources on the www.conversationsthatsell.com website.

My suggestion for utilizing technology is to use the tools your company provides to supplement your efforts. No tool is perfect, so extract what you can from what is available to you. If your company does not provide tools, then determine the tools that solve your main sales activity problems (tracking, data access, follow-up) and put them to work for you.

THE MOST IMPORTANT SALES TOOL: YOU!

Paper or power tools don't make sales. *You* do. You are the most important tool in your toolbox. Use your time, efforts, skills, and strengths effectively to gain higher efficiency, lower stress, higher productivity, greater happiness, and job security.

To best utilize your strengths, you need to know what they are. Regular assessment of your abilities and what works and doesn't work for you is a smart practice. Assessing your strengths for the Skill and Will factors discussed in Chapter 11 also provides a platform for you to build from.

There are two tools you can use to assess your strengths and weaknesses:

1. *The Tribal Types Tool.* Use the Tribal Types Tool as a personal assessment to identify how *your* customs impact your communication and collaborative selling activities. This knowledge explains why you do and don't engage in certain activities. For example, as an Achiever I don't enjoy detailed work, which causes me to procrastinate on some of the tedious but vital administrative work. My colleague, Anne Solomons of Touch Point Training Consultants, is an Expresser and doesn't like to do work that keeps her in the office and out of touch with people, so she finds ways to work people contact into every workday.

2. *The Sales Survey.* Use the Sales Survey at www.conversationsthatsell. com to identify your benchmark of the Skill and Will components. The results of the survey make it easy for you to capitalize on your strengths—and suggest which of the components you may want to develop further.

Use the information from your assessments to pinpoint your self-development opportunities. For maximum impact, choose two or three specific Skill and Will components from the assessments to focus your development efforts. A tip for you: Don't get caught in the trap of thinking you need to tackle the lowest scoring items. Often you will benefit more when you further develop your strengths and areas of moderate strength than if you pick the lowest scoring items.

Once you know where you want to focus your self-development efforts, you are ready for Chapter 13 and an easy-to-follow process that will help you achieve your goals.

* * *

The value of the tools in your toolbox is higher when you consistently incorporate the tools into how you manage your activities and prepare for your conversations. You will get more from your time and efforts and working smarter leaves you with more time and energy.

QUICK TIPS TO USE WHAT'S IN YOUR TOOLBOX

- Prepare for every conversation on paper. Use the WIIFT Quick Prep Tool as a guide to planning your conversation flow.

- Make time for researching new buyers, large opportunities, or stalled sales. The Quick Research guide provides thought-starters for where to begin your research.

- Use Tribal Types to adjust how you work and sell with your buyers.

- Stay current with the technology tools available to you for managing your sales activities and buyers. Then use what you have.

- Identify your benchmark for the Skill and Will factors. Keep doing what works well. For the components you want to build or change, use Chapter 13's goal-setting process to establish your growth development plan.

Now What? Action Time!

"A good plan today is better than a perfect plan tomorrow."
—PROVERB

Throughout this book I've mentioned how busy buyers are. Yet, you are busy too, aren't you? And that busy-ness leads to full days—mostly spent reacting to the demands of everyone else. To make sure you aren't lost in all the reactive activity, you need to be more purposeful with your time and actions. Ernest Hemingway wrote, "Never mistake motion for action." Even though you may put forth great effort and fill your days with activity, a scattershot approach is ineffective and benefits neither you nor your buyers.

Purposeful, focused action stems from knowing what to do with your *skill*, and then tapping into your *will* to do it. To help you identify the specific, purposeful actions that will get you where you want or need to be, this book ends with a guide to setting, planning for, and achieving your goals.

The goal achievement process outlined here will strengthen your Goal Transparency, one of the four Success Drivers discussed in Chapter 11, and lead to greater control of your time, energy, and activities.

TARGET YOUR SUCCESS WITH READY, AIM, SUCCEED

Though setting goals begins the process, there is a great deal more to goal achievement. With about thirty minutes of focus, you can significantly increase the likelihood of achieving your desired outcomes for the time period of your choice—a day, a month, six months, or a year.

Targeting your efforts narrows the number of things you need to focus on and lets you zone in on the most important activities for your success. This process works for any outcome or goal—from what you want to earn this year, to your health, to what you will do with the tips and tools in this book. The goal achievement process is designed for you to identify, plan, and execute; measure your progress; and celebrate your goal success. And while I can't promise you won't encounter roadblocks or speed bumps along the way (most of us do), you will have the opportunity to get where you want to be more easily and efficiently.

The goal achievement process is:

- *Get ready:* Do the preliminary work that ensures you set relevant goals.

- *Take aim:* Define the specific goal and make a solid plan to achieve it.

- *Act to succeed:* Identify your stakeholders, the resources you need, and the rewards for achieving your goal—your What's in it for *Me*; then follow with a regular review and update of your goals.

- *Celebrate:* Keep yourself energized to reach your goals.

GET READY

Getting started with setting goals can be difficult. Many people don't know what they want to achieve—or don't know how to articulate it. Top performers are the exception; they know and can articulate their goals.

Because goal achievement is so important, the process is included in all of my sales workshops. And at least 10 percent of participants struggle with the goal-setting element of the process. They tell me, "I don't know what I want," "My manager dictates my goals," "I have no control over the goals set for me," or "I can't set a goal because there is too much variability in my territory, life, income, etc."

This struggle with identifying a goal is common, according to Laura Goodrich, an authority in the field of workplace dynamics and relationships and author and producer of the video *Seeing Red Cars*. Her message that "you get more of whatever you focus on" plays out daily. When asked what they want, she says, most people tell you what they *don't* want. The pattern of focusing on what you don't want is widespread. To break that pattern, this chapter will guide you through identifying at least four goals for what you want to achieve, obtain, or deliver, with an initial plan to achieve them.

In thirty minutes or less, your goals will be set.

To help identify what is important to you—which will make it easier to set your goals and build them into a full goal plan—begin with the short list of thought-starter topics that follows. You will see that the topics are not all about work or sales. Your goals should connect your work and personal life into one cohesive focus.

Start the process by placing a checkmark in front of all major topics (listed below) that you want to focus on for a specific time period, or write them on a blank piece of paper.

- *Work:* earnings, production/sales, awards, role/promotion, new customers, schedule, territory, responsibilities, desired projects.

- *Financial:* milestone to reach, debt to reduce/bills to pay off, purchase to make, savings each month, earnings, retirement plans to fund.

- *Relationships:* Person/group you would like to have a relationship with, a relationship to improve, a relationship to end.

- *Health:* exercise, weight, bad habits to break, good habits to build, health concern to eliminate.

- *Learning:* courses to take, degrees to earn, books to read, conferences to attend, skills to build, hobbies to begin.

- *Rewards:* awards, recognition you want to earn, salary increase, bonus, trip.

- *Home/apartment:* upgrade, update, location, projects, organizing.

- *Leisure:* activities, events, use of time, relationships, trips to take.

Did any of these resonate with you and jump-start your thinking about what you want to focus on? If not, write in a topic of your choice.

Now review the selected topics and circle the specific items within each of these topics that are important to you. For example, if Health is checked, you might circle "good habits to build." If Rewards is checked, you could circle "bonus" as another important item.

The simple but effective Goal Planner™ shown in Figure 13–1 will guide you through the rest of the goal achievement elements. Complete the Get Ready step by photocopying this Goal Planner page or downloading a copy of the Goal Planner's online version from www.conversationsthatsell. com. You will need at least four copies, one for each goal, to finish this process. I suggest using a pencil to write so you can edit as needed. No goal is ever set in stone.

The Goal Planner outlines all the necessary elements for you to identify, plan, and execute your goals.

You are now ready to Take Aim and write your goal.

TAKE AIM

To clearly define your goal statement include *What* and *When.*

What is the result or outcome with measurement defined (i.e., closed sales, contracts signed, appointments set, etc). *When* is the Time/Date to achieve your result or outcome. If you can assign a date right now, great; if not, fill it in later.

Here are a few examples of goal statements that include *What* and *When* specifics:

- On 12/31/xx I have twelve contracts signed for $2.25 million of delivered product in January 20xx.

- By 9/1/xx, I exercise for a minimum of thirty minutes, four days a week.

- On 6/30/xx my six-month sales goal of $900,000 is reached.

- On 12/31/xx my annual income is $250,000.

Figure 13–1 Goal Planner™

Goal Planner™

Date: _____

Ready • • • A goal is a statement of the desired end result.

Aim • • •
My Goal (what and when)

Action • • •

Action Steps to reach my goal	Time/Date	Others Involved	Progress Notes

Weekly actions I will take to stay on target

Succeed • • •

Stakeholders   Resources (time, materials, people, money, etc.)

Metrics I will use to track progress and success.

Celebrate • • •
Reward/Benefits of achieving the goal (why)

Date Goal Achieved
(write debrief notes on back)

It is a good practice to break annual goals into shorter time frames for focus and accountability. Using the first example:

On 12/31/xx I have twelve contracts signed for $2.25 million of delivered product in January 20xx.

You can break down the goal into a shorter time frame:

I have four signed contracts for delivered product of $800,000 by 9/30/xx.

Three Tips for Creating Productive Goals

Ensure you are writing productive goals by following these three tips:

1. *Make the goal measurable and specific.* A specific goal allows you to know whether you've hit the bull's-eye or not.

    Identify the specifics such as dollars, number of accounts, prospects at certain points in your pipeline, appointments, a certain weight, a specific destination, etc.
    One common goal I often hear is, "I will spend more time with my family." A worthy outcome—but it isn't specific or measurable. What does "spending more time" mean? A specific amount of time each night or weekend? How will you know if that is achieved? What is the measurement?
    Make your goal specific: "I eat dinner with my family three times each week as of 7/1/xx." This specific and measurable statement allows you to track your progress and know whether you have achieved this goal.

2. *Set a realistic target.* Identify attainable outcomes. While the BHAG (big, hairy audacious goals) may look impressive, all of your goals should be within your reach. Are you really going to increase *this* by 75 percent or decrease *that* by 150 percent? Better to set a smaller increase or decrease, achieve that, and then build from it. The Weight Watchers® organization—with a system proven over decades—starts with a 10 percent goal because it is realistic. Once the 10 percent goal is achieved, a new goal is set.

Pay attention to your self-talk as you write your goal. If you are thinking or saying, "Yeah right," "I can *try* that," or "That's really a stretch," the goal is most likely unrealistic.

If you set your goal too high, your energy, confidence, and motivation to achieve it will wane. By setting a goal that is realistic and reachable, you will gain the momentum and confidence to achieve the outcome.

3. *Write the desired outcome in the present tense.* For example, use "I have" or "I am." Writing the outcome as if you have already achieved it puts you in the mindset that you can achieve it.

At this point don't get caught up with how you will achieve the goal. Focusing on the "how" can cause delays in setting it.

For each of the topics you selected earlier, write a goal statement in the "Aim" section on one of the four Planners. Use the three tips to ensure these goals are productive. Write them as a specific outcome you desire or need and include a time frame.

When you are finished writing at least one goal statement with the *What* and *When*, congratulations! You're now in the 10 percent of adults who actually have any goals in writing. Goal statements give a clear target to strive for and focus on. *Achieving* your goals requires more planning and action.

Identify Your Plan of Action

Planning the specific actions you will need to take to reach your goal is part of Take Aim. It's likely there are a variety of paths you could take and you will need to make some choices for the actions that will work for you.

Let's return to the example on page 206:

I have four signed contracts for delivered product of $800,000 by 9/30/xx.

There may be a dozen actions I could take to get the four contracts. I may need each of them—or maybe not. Identify the actions you commit to taking and that will work best for you.

For this example, "The actions I will take to achieve my goal include:

- Follow up with Prospects A, B, C, X, Y, Z about their outstanding pro-posals within ten days.

- Brainstorm with my manager as to how to approach my stalled sales for Prospects M, N. Make contact with those prospects.

- Schedule thirty minutes each morning to prepare for every meeting that day. Research new information and identify how to use it in my conversation.

To outline your specific action plan in the Action section of the Planner:

- In the left column on the Goal Planner under Actions, write all the pos-sible actions that will move you toward your goal.

- In the second column, add a specific time/date when you will take that action. Is it each day? Week? The action date is another checkpoint on your road to success.

- Determine who else is involved—whose help or buy-in is needed for different actions. Write these names in the third column under "Others."

You may have discovered you need eight actions, or maybe only two. Sometimes actions are robust and will become short-term goals themselves with their own outcome and actions.

To make this plan more specific and actionable, finish your planning by identifying the actions you will take *this* week to move toward these goals. Write those actions on the Goal Planner in the Weekly Actions section.

ACT TO SUCCEED

Your plan is now defined. Good for you! Is this a guarantee of reaching your goal on time, within budget, and with your sanity?

Realistically? No. Roadblocks (other priorities, market changes, etc.) might pop up, changing your direction. To succeed you need to tap into the power of stakeholders, plan your budget, take action, and update and con-firm your plan.

The Power of Stakeholders

A stakeholder is someone who cares about or is affected by the outcome of your goal. It might be a manager, a family member, a colleague, or a friend.

Sharing your goals with a stakeholder makes your goal transparent and provides accountability for you to reach it. It's much easier to delay working on a goal that no one else knows about. Knowing that your stakeholder will ask you about progress often provides the nudge to get moving on it. Additional stakeholder benefits include:

- Clarifying the outcome with you to make sure it is specific enough for you to know whether you reach it.

- Identifying other actions that can get you there quicker or easier and eliminate some of the roadblocks.

- Supporting you along the way.

- Contributing to resources or help with actions.

- Celebrating your progress and ultimate success!

Involving a stakeholder is a powerful way to increase the likelihood of achieving your goal. So why don't more people identify stakeholders and ask for their support? They tell me they don't want to burden someone else. Though understandable, they're overlooking the benefits a stakeholder receives from supporting or assisting them with their goals.

Stakeholders benefit with the sense of satisfaction from helping someone else succeed, a boost that helps them achieve a goal of their own (there is power in being with others who are succeeding and achieving), and an opportunity to learn or be exposed to something new.

You will succeed more easily when you find the right stakeholder for your goals. If the stakeholder you select doesn't want to be involved, that's okay. You'll find one who does.

To use myself as an example, I spend a lot of energy at work and usually enjoy the "break" from work when with my family. So when I was working on a huge, all-consuming international project, I didn't really want to share the project goals or outcomes outside of work. I did, however, share the details and struggles with my key stakeholder—my husband.

As a stakeholder he was able to provide support and understanding when I was locked in my office for hours after dinner. He even read the documents that I was stuck on and his outside perspective made for a better outcome. Of course, he also shared in the rewards of a successful project.

Plan Your "Budget"

Many goals are derailed because the resources necessary to achieve them—money, time, people, or supplies—were not considered or budgeted. Resource demands that creep up can create an impasse and waste time and energy as the goal is significantly delayed or abandoned. Knowing the resources needed to reach your goal helps you stay realistic.

For example, if the goal is "Purchase a new vehicle by August 1," you may find:

- Resources are more available than you first thought.

- Interest rates are in your favor and you can actually make the purchase by June 30.

- Your trade-in is worth less than you thought and October 1 is more realistic.

Identifying the resources upfront ensures you have the right time frame and plan to succeed. If they don't match up, now is the time to adjust them. Review your resources each time you complete a goal checkup.

List the necessary resources in the Goal Planner. Adjust your outcome, stakeholders, and time frame as necessary to work within the available resources.

TAKE ACTION, AND UPDATE
AND CONFIRM YOUR PLAN

Identifying or setting goals can be hard. *Acting* on the plan is harder, and committing to the plan consistently to achieve the goal is harder still.

It's easy to start second-guessing or wanting to tweak your plan or strive for the elusive "perfect plan." This can cause delays and may kill your ability to achieve your goals. At some level of "rightness," it's time for you to stop working on putting your plan together and start taking action to achieve the goal.

As I said in my blog at www.salesproductivityinsider.com (July 26, 2012), "Successful sellers take action when others don't and take actions that others won't."

Action means productively moving forward, not just filling your days. To achieve your goals, act on the activities you have outlined and then regularly review, update, and confirm your plan. This checkup ensures you are acting on the things that are most relevant and timely.

A common misconception about setting goals is that a written goal is set in stone and must be met as originally outlined. Not true! Every day brings new considerations that may affect the goal itself or the path to reaching it. That is why an effective goal achievement process includes the opportunity to review your goals, adjusting your priorities, plan, and time frame as needed.

One of my favorite examples of this is when I was working through a review of my goals with a colleague. I was frustrated because I had not made *any* progress on one specific goal that I had in place for the previous three years.

My colleague asked me the following questions: "If you haven't done anything about this goal in three years, how important is it to you? Does it belong as one of the six goals you are focusing on right now?"

My response was slow in coming because I had never considered that question. Then I blurted out, "Well, I guess it mustn't be important or I would have done something about it by now, right?"

He responded, "Then why is it is one of your goals?"

I said, "Because someone told me I needed to learn to golf if I was going to succeed in business. So I made it a goal." (Yes, becoming a proficient golfer was a goal of mine for three years.)

He laughed and said, "You seem to be doing fine in business without golfing. It's okay to replace that goal with something more meaningful."

Wow! I had permission to *remove* and *replace* a goal. Instead of feeling like a failure whenever I reviewed my goals and recognized my lack of progress on it, I was able to decide that the goal wasn't that important to me. The relief I felt was huge.

Years later, I'm still not a good golfer and my business has grown every year. Thank goodness I had someone who was willing to ask me questions to help me clarify the why and what of my goals.

Regular checkups also allow you to acknowledge and celebrate progress or make the necessary adjustments to achieve your goals. The 4R's for goal reviews work well: Review, Renew, Revise, or Replace.

- *Review:* Read your goals and the plan to achieve them. Use metrics to gauge your progress. Are you on track? If yes, move to Renew. Not on track? Revise or Replace.

- *Renew:* Recommit yourself to the goal and the time frame. Consciously think through the next action steps and how you will feel when the goal is accomplished. Note your progress.

- *Revise:* If the situation has changed, revise your goal as needed. Maybe the timing is off, the outcome needs to be edited, or the people involved have changed. It's okay to make those revisions to create a realistic goal relevant to *today* for you.

- *Replace:* Remove and replace a goal if it no longer fits. Just because a goal made sense when you wrote it doesn't mean it still makes sense today. It's okay to replace a goal with one that is more meaningful and timely. Use a new Goal Planner to identify and plan for the new goal.

Update your stakeholders after each 4R checkup. They need to know your goal progress to be effective.

Determine how often you will use the 4R's to stay on track—at least monthly is recommended. Then schedule thirty minutes on your calendar for this checkup.

CELEBRATE!

You have gotten *Ready*; taken *Aim* and planned for action; prepared and taken action to *Succeed*; and now it's time to identify the Why for your goals—the What's in it for *You*—and *Celebrate* progress and success.

Defining the Why illuminates the reward or the benefit of achieving your goals. A specific reward is more motivating and more likely to drive you to take the necessary action.

Often I hear people say their reward is to earn more. But is that the *real* reward, the real What's in it for *You*? What does that extra money do for you? Is it to buy something, pay off debt, or give your family something specific? Rewards are unique to each person. Identify a specific reward or *What's in it for You* for each goal. Whether big or small, make the rewards relevant and something that helps drive you to achieve the goal.

These rewards could be a dinner at a special restaurant with your spouse or significant other, a day of biking with the club, a golf event with a friend, a day off from working out, an ice cream treat, quiet time to read a book, a "happy dance" (one of my favorites), or your name on a plaque or trophy.

The reward needs to be important enough for you to want to achieve the goal. Broad rewards are a good start, for example:

- Get my boss off my back.

- Keep my job.

- Feel good.

- Have less stress.

- Enjoy better health.

And finally, it's important to take the time to pause and celebrate. Take time to pay yourself the reward you identified. As an Achiever, I don't pause enough when I complete a goal. I move right into the next one. Thank goodness my stakeholders stop me and hold me accountable to celebrate.

If you want to increase your motivation to complete the necessary actions, find ways to celebrate progress, not just the final outcome. Don't hold out on acknowledging your progress or success because you are so focused on what isn't yet done. That trap will drain your energy. Find ways to enjoy your journey and acknowledge or celebrate the milestones along the way.

* * *

There you have it, an easy-to-follow process to achieve what *you* want.

Each element of the process is important and probably easier than you might think. Use the Goal Planner to guide you through the specific elements. The key is to get started.

I've given you a lot of information about how to skillfully and willfully have conversations that count. And although information is powerful, it is only powerful when put to good use. To ensure you benefit from the time you invested in reading the book, I end with a quote by Walt Disney: "The way to get started is to quit talking and begin doing."

QUICK TIPS TO ACHIEVE YOUR GOALS

- Set a realistic goal. Include the *What* and *When* of the goal and write the goal in the "now" (as if you were already "there").

- Commit to the goal, verbally and in writing.

- Identify the *Why*—your real reward for achieving the goal.

- Share with a stakeholder.

- Take action! Find something every day (or at least weekly) that moves you forward.

- Acknowledge the roadblocks that pop up, work through them, or revise your plan around them.

- Celebrate your progress and final destination. Don't just wait for the final end result; enjoy the progress points along the way.

- Use the 4R's checkup process at regular intervals, monthly is recommended, to keep your goal achievement on track: *Review* your goal; *Renew* your commitment; *Revise* the goal as needed; *Replace* unnecessary goals.

INDEX